CULTURES OF THE WORLD

GRENADA

Guek-Cheng Pang

MARSHALL CAVENDISH
New York • London • Sydney

Reference edition reprinted 2001 by
Marshall Cavendish Corporation
99 White Plains Road
Tarrytown
New York 10591

Originated and designed by
Times Books International, an imprint of
Times Media Private Limited, a member of the
Times Publishing Group

Printed in Malaysia

Library of Congress Cataloging-in-Publication Data:

Cheng, Pang Guek, 1950-
    Grenada / Pang Guek Cheng.
        p. cm. — (Cultures of the World)
    ISBN 0-7614-1160-7
    1. Grenada—Juvenile literature. [1. Grenada.] I. Title.
II. Series.

F2056 .C45 2001
972.9845—dc21
                        00-047583
                    CIP
                    AC

INTRODUCTION

Grenada? Is this place in Spain? Is it the place the Americans invaded? These are two responses one gets when the subject of Grenada arises. Not many people know anything about this beautiful island in the Caribbean, which explains why it has remained so relatively unspoiled even today.

But to learn about Grenada is to discover a place of great natural beauty, of verdant volcanic hillsides ringed by miles of spotless white and black sand beaches. Grenada was shaped by a complex history and was often a pawn in the wars of other nations. The country experienced the hardships of slavery and survived the mass migrations of its people. A quiet place, it was relatively unknown until a revolution in 1983 caused it to be the only Caribbean nation to be invaded by the United States.

Cultures of the World: Grenada also discovers a people who are proud to be black, proud to be Caribbean, and most of all, proud to be Grenadian.

CONTENTS

Colorful boats brighten up the dock of a sailing club.

3 INTRODUCTION

7 GEOGRAPHY
The Caribbean islands • Balmy all year • Rainfall • Topography • Lakes and beaches • Rainforests • Flora • Fauna • French-built towns • Grenada's sister islands

21 HISTORY
Grenada on the map • Gold lures Europeans • Early colonization • Britain wins Grenada • Slaves and revolts • The road to freedom • Emancipation • Immigration • Freedom to vote

33 GOVERNMENT
Federation fails • Unions • Road to self-government • British-style government • Revolution • Six-day invasion • The 1990 elections • Keeping the peace

45 ECONOMY
Agriculture • Spices • Fishing • Tourism • Small industries • Over land and sea

53 GRENADIANS
Indigenous people • Slavery • Plantation life • Indentured labor • The people today

61 LIFESTYLE
Village rhythms • Market day • Transportation • Grenadian women • The family unit • A traditional Grenadian wedding • Rituals of death • Birth • Health • Education

73 RELIGION
Arrival of the Dominicans • Four main Christian churches • Traditional beliefs • Rastas

CONTENTS

79 LANGUAGE
Creole English • The French connection • The media

85 ARTS
Calypso • Musical instruments • Folk dances • Warm climate, vibrant colors • Folk artists • Grenadian handicrafts • Theater and literature

95 LEISURE
Cricket • Soccer • Water sports • Other leisure activities • Children's games • Relaxing with rum • Nightlife • Folk tales

107 FESTIVALS
Carnival • Feast days • Parang • Big Drum • Maroons • Boat launching festival

113 FOOD
Ground provisions • Roti and rice • Isle of spice • The pepper pot • Refreshing drinks • Rum

122 MAP OF GRENADA

124 QUICK NOTES

125 GLOSSARY

126 BIBLIOGRAPHY

126 INDEX

A modern Grenadian woman.

GEOGRAPHY

GRENADA ("GRE-NAY-DA") IS AN ISLAND in the Caribbean Sea. It is part of an archipelago of over 7,000 islands, many of them nothing more than little rocky outcrops poking above the surface of the ocean.

The nation of Grenada consists of the island of Grenada itself, which is about 21 miles (34 km) long and 12 miles (19 km) wide at its widest part, and the smaller islands of Carriacou ("Carri-ah-KOO") and Petit Martinique ("Petty Mar-ti-NEEK") plus more than 20 small islands or cays ("KEYS").

The three main islands are very small. Carriacou lies 23 miles (37km) northeast of Grenada. Petit Martinique is another 5 miles (8 km) northeast of Carriacou. The three islands have a total land mass of 140 square miles (363 square km). Grenada is 120 square miles (311 square km), about twice the size of Washington, D.C., while Carriacou is 13 square miles (34 square km), and Petit Martinique is 486 acres (197 hectares).

Left: **A stream created by an islet of coral.**

Opposite: **Surrounded by water, Grenada is a beautiful country blessed with a tropical climate all year.**

THE CARIBBEAN ISLANDS

The Caribbean islands lie south of Florida, separating the Caribbean Sea to the west from the Atlantic Ocean to the east. The largest islands in the group—Cuba, Jamaica, Hispaniola, and Puerto Rico—make up the Greater Antilles. North of these four large islands is the Bahamas.

The islands of the Lesser Antilles lie to the east and south of Puerto Rico. The Lesser Antilles are divided into two groups: the Leeward Islands and the Windward Islands. The Windward Islands are Dominica, Martinique, St. Lucia, St. Vincent, the Grenadines, and Grenada and its adjacent islands, while the Leeward Islands include those between Anguilla and Guadeloupe and their adjacent islands. Finally, there is the group of islands closest to the Venezuelan coast: Trinidad and Tobago, Aruba, Bonaire, and Curaçao.

Geologists believe that during the last Ice Age, all the Caribbean islands formed a land bridge that linked Florida with Venezuela. But this land mass was submerged by the sea in a series of earthquakes and volcanic eruptions so that only the tops of the mountains remain as islands today.

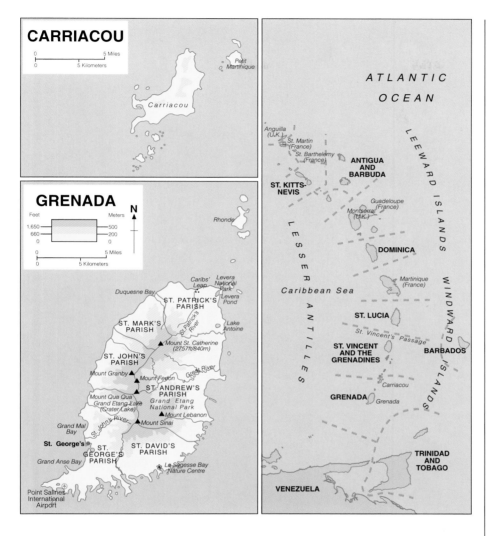

CARRIACOU

| 0 | 5 Miles |
| 0 | 5 Kilometers |

Petit
Martinique

Carriacou

GRENADA   N

Feet		Meters
1,650		500
660		200
0		0
0	5 Miles	
0	5 Kilometers	

Caribs'
Leap
Levera
National
Park
Duquesne Bay
Levera
Pond
ST. PATRICK'S
PARISH
St. Patrick's River
ST. MARK'S
PARISH
Lake
Antoine
Mount St. Catherine
(2757ft/840m)
ST. JOHN'S
PARISH
Mount Granby
Great River
Mount Fedon
ST. ANDREW'S
PARISH
Mount Qua Qua
Grand Etang Lake
(Crater Lake)
Grand Etang
National Park
Mount Lebanon
St. John's River
Mount Sinai
Grand Mal
Bay
St. George's
ST.
GEORGE'S
PARISH
ST. DAVID'S
PARISH
Grand Anse Bay
La Sagesse Bay
Nature Centre
Point Salines
International
Airport

ATLANTIC
OCEAN

Anguilla
(U.K.)
St. Martin
(France)
St. Barthélemy
(France)
ANTIGUA
AND
BARBUDA
ST. KITTS-
NEVIS
Guadeloupe
(France)
Montserrat
(U.K.)
Rhonde
L E E W A R D   I S L A N D S
L E S S E R   A N T I L L E S
DOMINICA
Caribbean Sea
Martinique
(France)
ST. LUCIA
St. Vincent's Passage
ST. VINCENT
AND THE
GRENADINES
BARBADOS
W I N D W A R D   I S L A N D S
Carriacou
GRENADA   Grenada
TRINIDAD
AND
TOBAGO
VENEZUELA

The most
destructive
hurricane in the
island's recorded
history was
Hurricane Janet,
which hit Grenada
on September 22,
1955.

BALMY ALL YEAR ROUND

Lying south of the Tropic of Cancer, Grenada has a warm climate all year. The temperature difference between the coolest months of the year, from December to March, and between the hottest months, August to November, is little more than 46°F to 50°F (8°C to 10°C). The average daily temperature is 80°F (27°C). Although the Caribbean is in the hurricane belt, Grenada is less affected than other islands by these destructive winds. Many heavy thunderstorms pass over Grenada during the hurricane season.

RAINFALL

Instead of summer and winter, Grenada has wet and dry seasons. The dry season is from January to March when the hills turn brown from lack of rain and rivers are low. The heaviest rainfall comes during the months of June to December, making the land green once more.

The highest rainfall occurs in the central mountains, which receive an average of 160 inches (406 cm) a year. The coastal regions are drier, getting about 50 inches (127 cm) a year, especially on the leeward side of the island. The southern tip is the driest part of the island. Grenada also receives convectional rain. This occurs when the land heats up during the day. This heats the air, which rises and creates a powerful updraft. As the air rises, it cools, and the moisture it contains is released as rain. This rain often falls in mid-afternoon.

HURRICANES

Hurricanes are a significant climactic phenomenon in the Caribbean. In the summer, strong winds develop in troughs of low pressure in the eastern Caribbean, bringing unsettled, overcast weather, often accompanied by heavy rains. Sometimes these winds gather enough force to become a hurricane. The term "hurricane" comes from a Carib word, *huracan* ("HU-rah-cahn"). It refers to a tropical storm with heavy rain and winds that exceed 74 mph (119 km/h). These high-velocity winds blow in a counterclockwise direction around a low pressure center, known as the eye of the storm, where the winds are calm. Yet the strongest winds rage most fiercely at the point closest to the eye. As the hurricane roars through, the area affected by the storm may be more than 150 miles (241 km) wide. The hurricane season is from June to November, with the greatest occurrence in August and September. On average, about five to eight hurricanes develop a year, but many fizzle out before they reach land.

The impressive Concord
Falls plunges 33 feet (10
m) into a pool.

TOPOGRAPHY

Like its sister Windward Islands, Grenada has a rich and varied terrain.
There are high mountains, rainforests, deep river valleys, beautiful lakes,
some desert-like areas, strings of beautiful white and black sand beaches,
and deep, sheltered harbors.

The highest peak is Mount St. Catherine, which is 2,757 feet (840 m)
high. Other mountains on the island—Mount Granby, Mount Lebanon,
and Mount Sinai—rise more than 2,000 feet (609 m) above sea level.

A number of rivers begin in the central mountains and flow to the sea.
Grenadians may call the same river by many names, depending on which
part of the country or which village it passes through. Major rivers include
the Great River that flows through the parish of St. Andrew, as well as St.
John's River, and St. Patrick's River.

The impressive Concord
Falls plunges 33 feet (10
m) into a pool.

LAKES AND BEACHES

There is much evidence on the island of the remains of volcanic activity—volcanic vents, black sand beaches, and sulfurous springs, especially on the north coast. Several extinct volcanic craters are now filled with beautiful lakes, such as Levera Pond and Lake Antoine in the northeast, and Grand Etang Lake in the center of the island.

Grand Etang Lake is 1,740 feet (530 m) above sea level. The area around it is a national park and a forest reserve. The park can be easily reached by road and by paths that allow visitors to enjoy the thick natural rainforest that surrounds the crater. Lake Antoine is just 20 feet (6 m) above sea level and is 16 acres (6 hectares) in size. It was formed 12,000 to 15,000 years ago during Grenada's final stage of volcanic activity.

The Grenadian coastline, which stretches for more than 80 miles (129 km), is indented by many beautiful bays and lovely beaches. The two most spectacular beaches are on the southern tip of the island—the Beach of Pines and the Grand Anse.

RAINFORESTS

There is a wide variety of natural vegetation on the island: lush tropical rainforests, woodlands, mangrove swamps, and desert scrub land.

Tropical rainforests flourish on the windward side of the mountains. About 160 inches (406 cm) of rain can fall in a year in the sheltered valleys there. Trees that grow more than 100 feet (30 m) tall are covered with mosses and ferns. Seasonal rainforests grow in slightly drier areas. They originally covered most of the lowland regions and can still be found on the leeward side of the island. Dry forests grow in regions that receive between 30 to 50 inches (76 to 127 cm) of rain a year. Trees that grow here are rarely more than 30 feet (9 m) tall and lose their leaves in the dry season.

Where people have cleared the forests, they have left flat, dry savannah grassland with scrub trees. Thorny trees and cactus scrub grow on the dry, leeward coasts. Mangrove swamps, trees, and shrubs that can survive in shallow and muddy salt water, cover some coastal areas.

All plant and animal life in the Caribbean migrated to the islands from the mainland of Venezuela, up through Trinidad and Tobago, the Lesser Antilles, and across the Greater Antilles to Puerto Rico, Hispaniola, Jamaica, and Cuba.

Above: **A dried nutmeg.**

Right: **Blossoming flowers add more color to the already beautiful Grand Etang National Park.**

FLORA

The tropical climate supports a vast number of economically useful trees. Fruit trees such as mango, papaya, and soursop are grown everywhere. There are palm trees of many kinds—date palms, queen palms, royal palms, and the coconut palm. The coconut palm is extremely useful—it provides food, drink, oil for cooking, and building materials.

Other common trees are the banyan, mahogany, and the calabash. Banyans are large trees with spreading branches and roots that hang from the branches to the ground. The mahogany, a native of the Caribbean, is valued for its wood. Calabash trees have large round fruit with hard shells that can be hollowed out and made into bowls, utensils, and craft objects.

Beautiful flowering plants, including orchids, ginger, hyacinth, bougainvillea, hibiscus, allamanda, frangipani, and oleander are found everywhere. The bougainvillea is Grenada's national flower.

FAUNA

When the Europeans arrived in the 15th century, they discovered limited animal life because few animals had been able to cross the water from South America. They did find bats and rodents, including the hutia, a large and tasty animal that reminded the Spanish of the rabbit.

The mongoose is commonly found in Grenada. It was brought by sugarcane farmers to help get rid of the cane rat. But the mongoose, being a daytime hunter, was not much help in killing the nocturnal rat. Instead, it became a nuisance, preying on other small island animals.

The mongoose preys on fish, chickens, crabs, and other small island animals.

There are several varieties of reptiles, including the caiman, snakes, and lizards. The iguana, which can grow to 5 feet (1.5 m) or more in length, is hunted by some who consider it a delicacy. But the iguana has fallen prey to the mongoose. There are no poisonous snakes or insects on the island. Troops of Mona monkeys, introduced from West Africa centuries ago, live in the forested areas.

There are many kinds of birds, butterflies, and insects. The Grenada dove is Grenada's national bird. There are bananaquits, hummingbirds, swifts, wrens, flycatchers, thrushes, finches, and blackbirds. Thousands of other birds stop over on the island on their migratory route from the north.

The seas are rich in marine life. The tropical fish are plentiful and colorful. There are grouper, snapper, angelfish, parrot fish, wrasse, and other reef inhabitants. The sea turtle comes ashore during March to August to lay its eggs. There are several species—the green turtle, leatherback, loggerhead, olive ridley, and the hawksbill. Turtles are sometimes sold in the fish market because some people love to eat turtle meat. But hunting laws protect them during certain times of the year.

The buildings that dot the Carenage are an architectural blend of French colonial, English Georgian, and Victorian.

FRENCH-BUILT TOWNS

The capital of Grenada is St. George's. About 11,000 people live and work in this town, which is on the south end of the island on a mile-long (0.6 km) peninsula. St. George's almost landlocked harbor, which is the crater of an extinct volcano, is so sheltered and deep that huge ocean liners are able to dock there.

The waterfront, known as the Carenage ("CA-reh-nagh") has pink, ocher, and brick-red commercial buildings and warehouses, many dating from the 18th century. The town was designed by the French governor, M. de Bellair, in 1705, and planning was continued by the British when they took control of the island. A ridge divides St. George's into two parts that are joined by the Sendall Tunnel, a 10-foot-wide (3 m) tunnel constructed in 1894.

Grenville, an agricultural town, is the second largest city in Grenada and the main port on the east coast. It is a regional center for collecting cocoa, nutmeg, and other agricultural products. It was established in 1763 by the

16

French, who called it La Baye. Victoria Street, the main street facing the waterfront, is the focus of the town's activity.

Gouyave is the main town of St. John's parish. Many of the residents here make their living from fishing. It is surrounded by nutmeg estates. The nutmeg processing station is the town's largest building.

GRENADA'S SISTER ISLANDS

Both Carriacou and Petit Martinique are part of the Grenadines, a chain of smaller islands that form a link between the larger island of Grenada in the south, and St. Vincent in the north. Carriacou and Petit Martinique are administered by Grenada, while the other Grenadines are run by the island of St. Vincent. The administrative line is so arbitrary that if one were to stand on the northern tip of Carriacou, at Rapid Point, one would actually be standing on St. Vincent territory. There are no rivers on Carriacou or Petit Martinique. The residents have to collect rain water in cisterns during the rainy season of June to December.

CARRIACOU The island of Carriacou, a name taken from a Carib word meaning "land of reefs," has a population of about 8,000. Like Grenada, it has a central mountainous region that slopes down to the coasts. But like Petit Martinique, it has a drier climate with an average annual rainfall of about 45 inches (114 cm).

The earliest European settlers on the island were the French who cleared the land and planted crops. Later the inhabitants of the island of Guadeloupe in the north arrived. When the British took control of the island in the 18th century, they grew cotton, sugarcane, coffee, cocoa, and indigo.

The smaller town of Windward is known for the shipwrights who came from Glasgow to build ships for the planters to transport the island's produce. Their descendants, bearing such Scottish names as McDonald, McLaren, MacFarland, and McLaurence, continue the tradition of building fishing boats and schooners today. Many families on Carriacou can also trace their ancestry to Africa and have also retained many of their African traditions.

PETIT MARTINIQUE The much smaller island of Petit Martinique, where about 600 people live, is one of many volcanic cones forming islands in the Caribbean. The island was settled by French fishermen who built their own boats for fishing. Most of the men on the island today are fishermen, while some work on regional ships.

Grenada has other smaller island dependencies in the Grenadine Islands that lie between the island of Grenada and Carriacou, such as Ile de Ronde, Kick-em Jenny, Green Bird, and Conference.

NATIONAL PARKS

Grenada has a few pristine natural areas that have been preserved. The Levera National Park on the northeast coast has dry woodland vegetation and a saltwater lagoon with a white sand beach. The lagoon is sheltered by coral reefs with mangrove swamps on either side. The La Sagesse Bay Nature Center along the southeast coast has mangroves, coral reefs, and dry woodlands. The largest national park on Grenada is the Grand Etang National Park, which covers the most mountainous central region of the island. Mount St. Catherine, Grenada's highest mountain, and Mount Qua Qua and Mount Fedon are the jewels of the park. Crater Lake, which is in the crater of an extinct volcano, is a 13-acre (5-hectare) expanse of cobalt-blue water. Visitors can hike in the park, using the many nature trails that have been developed.

HISTORY

THE CARIBBEAN WAS INHABITED BY SEVERAL GROUPS of people long before Christopher Columbus arrived in the area in 1492 and first put it on the map. The earliest people came from the mainland of South America and are collectively called Amerindians.

There were three groups of Amerindians. The first was the little-known Ciboneys. Their name, meaning "stone people," was given to them by the next group of people who arrived, the Arawaks. The Arawaks, a peaceful people with an advanced civilization, lived on fish and cassava. Their petroglyphs can be seen in north Grenada. A fierce and war-like race of Amerindians arrived next. They raided the Arawak villages, killed the men, and enslaved the women. When the Europeans arrived there, they called these people Caribs, and the area became known as the Caribees. From this comes the name Caribbean.

Left: **A representation of the earliest Amerindians. They covered their heads, necks, arms, private parts, and feet with feathers, and the men had precious stones on their faces. The people also fought with and ate each other. The body parts of those who were slain were hung in smoke.**

Opposite: **The remains of an old sugar mill in Carriacou. Sugarcane was the first cash crop cultivated in Grenada.**

Christopher Columbus returning to Spain to report his great discovery to Queen Isabella.

GRENADA ON THE MAP

The Caribbean was first placed on the map in 1492 when the Spanish adventurer Christopher Columbus chanced on the Bahamas, landing on San Salvador, known as Watling's Island. He was searching for a westward passage to the East Indies. He explored the Bahamas, the north coast of Cuba, and reached the northeastern tip of another large island that he named Isla Española, known today as Hispaniola. Leaving some men behind to establish a small settlement, Columbus returned to Spain to report his discovery.

In 1498, on his third trip to the Caribbean, Columbus arrived at the north of Grenada, then called Camerhogne by the Amerindians. He named the island Concepción. The name was changed to Granada on 16th century maps because the green hills reminded the Spanish sailors of Granada in Spain. The French, who settled on the island in the 1600s, changed the name to Grenade. When the British took possession of the island in 1763, the island became known as Grenada.

GOLD LURES EUROPEANS

Columbus' exciting discovery opened the floodgates of European exploitation. Over the next few centuries the Caribbean islands were pawns in a game of power among the Spanish, French, British, and Dutch.

Spain's interest was mainly centered on the islands of Cuba, Jamaica, and Puerto Rico as gold could be found on them. Natives were forced to work in the gold mines until the gold was exhausted. The Arawak population was decimated, while the Caribs survived by retreating to the mountainous interiors and fighting back with some success.

When more gold were discovered in Peru and Mexico, the islands lost their importance. Spanish ships were attacked by English and French pirates. The Dutch entered the fray later. They wanted the high-grade salt of Venezuela and the tobacco, which was becoming popular in Europe.

After years of plundering Spanish possessions, the northern Europeans established their colonies in the Caribbean in the 1600s. Possession of the islands changed hands according to the fortunes of wars in Europe.

The British "Vanguard" attacking Spanish ships in an attempt to capture their goods.

23

EARLY COLONIZATION

The first colonies were run by merchants authorized by their governments to represent them. When they became economic burdens, the French government sold the islands to the merchant-governors.

The Caribs resisted early colonization attempts by the Europeans. In 1650 two Frenchmen bought St. Lucia, Grenada, and the Grenadines. Hostilities soon broke out. Three years later the French governor of Guadeloupe sent a force to Grenada that overran and killed the Caribs, finally cornering the last few in the north of the island. Rather than surrender, the remaining 40 Carib men, women, and children leaped off a cliff to their deaths. The cliff is now called Leapers' Bluff.

The island then continued to change hands over the next two decades. After the Treaty of Utrecht in 1713 that ended the War of the Spanish Succession, the Caribbean enjoyed almost 80 years of peace and prosperity.

BRITAIN WINS GRENADA

In 1762 the British fleet sailed for Grenade and took it easily without even firing one shot. They promptly renamed the island Grenada. This victory was formalized in 1763 by the Treaty of Paris.

By this treaty Britain gained control over St. Vincent, Dominica, Grenada, and Tobago. Thousands of adventurers from the British Isles immediately sailed for the Caribbean. They cleared the forests, planted cane, built sugar mills, and imported thousands of slaves from Africa.

The new sugar plantations thrived on St. Vincent and Grenada until they were devastated by slave rebellions in 1795. In 1779, when the British fleet left the Caribbean to accompany some merchant ships to Britain, the French captured St. Vincent. They sailed for Grenada and repossessed it after a two-day battle. But under the Treaty of Versailles signed in 1783, Grenada once again returned to British hands.

The River Antoine Rum Distillery was built in 1763. It houses one of the last remaining water-driven cane-crushers. During its peak Grenada was England's fourth largest producer of sugar.

Above: **Fort George, situated above the harbor of St. George's, was built in the early 18th century by the French. At that time it was called Fort Royal.**

Opposite: **Slaves on the slave ship, *Wildfire*, which was on its way to the United States. The slaves in the Caribbean gained their freedom sooner, and with far less bloodshed and bitterness, than those in the United States.**

SLAVES AND REVOLTS

During the French occupation, the British settlers were treated badly. So when the British took control, the French suffered. The French eventually rebeled. Led by Julien Fedon, a Grenadian planter of African and French ancestry, thousands of slaves and free colored had the British on the run for more than a year.

Simultaneous slave revolts on many islands made it difficult for the British to rule in the Caribbean. Britain sent 17,000 troops to the Windward Islands in 1796 and ultimately did retake the islands, but only after meeting with fierce resistance.

Meanwhile, the number of slaves in proportion to Europeans was rising. The white population decreased because there was no work for wage laborers. White settlers preferred to emigrate to North America in search of jobs. The planters became increasingly dependent on their slaves, training them to be servants, drivers, and even bookkeepers and managers of their estates.

THE ROAD TO FREEDOM

Until the late 1700s European governments and statesmen believed that slavery was inevitable if they were to benefit from valuable exports like sugar and other tropical products. But the political thinking was slowly changing.

Many began to realize that slavery was wrong. They forced planters in their colonies to abolish slavery. Emancipation in Grenada was gained with great difficulty, and more than 25 years passed between the end of the slave trade in 1808 and the abolition of slavery in 1834.

In 1806 Britain banned the sale of slaves to foreign colonies. One year later, the import of slaves into British colonies was outlawed. The end of the slave trade finally came in 1808.

The increasing number of slave rebellions after 1815 strongly influenced public opinion in Britain. The Abolition of Slavery Act was passed in August 1833, ordering the end of slavery in 1834. Emancipation took a longer time to take effect because the slaves were forced into a period of apprenticeship. It was only on August 1, 1838, at midnight, that the 750,000 slaves in the British colonies became free. There were celebrations, parades, and thanksgiving in the churches. For most slaves, freedom meant the right to live as a self-reliant small farmer.

SLAVE TRADE

The coastal exploration of Africa and the invasion of the Americas by the Europeans in the 15th century gave rise to the slave trade. Portugal was the first European nation to begin importing slaves. The Portuguese imported hundreds of slaves to Portugal from trading posts and forts on the African coast to meet labor needs. The slaves were captured by other Africans and brought to the coast. Spain soon followed, when the native populations of Latin America, who were forced to work on the plantations, could not survive the harsh conditions of slavery and died. This is partly because of exposure to European diseases as well as the hard labor. England entered the slave trade in the second half of the 16th century, fighting with Portugal to supply the Spanish colonies with slaves. In1713 the British South Sea Company was given exclusive right to supply the Spanish colonies with slaves. Other countries—France, Holland, Denmark and the American colonies themselves—soon entered this lucrative business. Denmark was the first European country to abolish the slave trade in 1792, followed by Britain in 1808. In 1814, at the Congress of Vienna, Britain convinced nearly all the other foreign powers to adopt a similar policy, and finally all European states passed laws to prohibit the slave trade. In 1842 Britain and the United States signed the Ashburton Treaty in which both countries agreed to maintain a squadron on the African coast to enforce the prohibition of the trade.

EMANCIPATION

Emancipation brought with it social and political difficulties. It increased a planter's costs at a time when sugar prices were falling. World production of sugar had increased dramatically, and the Caribbean islands had to compete with other sugar producing regions. Beet sugar was also a cheap substitute for cane sugar.

The freed slaves were no longer willing to work in the sugar fields. They had each been given a small plot of land on which to grow their food and sell whatever surplus they might have. Most of them became independent farmers. When they did work on the estates, they were no longer submissive or willing to be cheap labor. The production of sugar for export stopped on the islands of Grenada, St. Vincent, Dominica, Tobago, and Montserrat. By 1856 most of the sugar estates in Grenada had been abandoned, and attention was switched to the planting of cocoa trees.

IMMIGRATION

New immigrants from Africa, India, and China arrived to fill the gaps left by the freed slaves. From 1846 to 1847, Portuguese workers arrived from the island of Madeira. But after 1850 most of the immigrants were indentured laborers from India, who came to work on the farms. Between 1838 and 1917, thousands of East Indian laborers arrived in Grenada.

By 1763 Grenada had a system of representative government, in which a governor ruled with the help of a council that had limited powers. An elected assembly of officials made local laws. In 1877 Grenada was made a Crown Colony, and the elected House of Assembly was replaced by the government in London. This was done to protect the British population from black majority rule.

Opposite: **After emancipation, most of the slaves gathered to cultivate a shared plot of land. Many of their descendants still own the land today.**

29

Queen Elizabeth II during her visit to Grenada in 1985.

FREEDOM TO VOTE

Emancipation meant that the former slaves were now free British citizens with a right to vote if they had the same qualifications as the whites. Voters often had only to own a small amount of property to qualify. This allowed many blacks to vote in legislative elections.

Although the unrepresentative governments slowed the islands' route to self-government, they nevertheless were competent in maintaining public order and providing public services. There was little incentive to work for economic growth, and the island economies stagnated.

In 1886 the colonial office in Britain united the islands of Grenada, St. Vincent, St. Lucia, and Tobago under the rule of one governor. Each island, however, had its own legislative council, police, judiciary, treasury, and public services. It was in 1974 that Grenada finally gained independence.

IMPORTANT DATES

8 B.C.–1 B.C.	Ciboneys settled in Grenada.
A.D. 1–1000	Arawaks made Grenada their home.
A.D. 1000–1650	Caribs lived on the island.
1498	Columbus sighted Grenada.
1609	First attempted settlement by British merchants.
1638	French under Monsieur de Poincy attempted settlement.
1650	Du Parquet, French governor of Martinique, purchased and established a settlement on Grenada.
1651–52	French-Carib War.
1763	Grenada ceded to the British by Treaty of Paris.
1771	Fire swept St. George.
1775	Second fire swept St. George.
1779	Island recaptured by the French.
1783	Grenada restored to British rule.
1791	Completion of forts at Richmond Hill and establishment of Market Square.
1792	One third of St. George's destroyed by fire.
1834	Emancipation.
1838	End of apprenticeship period.
1912	Arrival of the automobile.
1955	Hurricane Janet.
1979	People's Revolutionary Government takes over.
1983	U.S. invasion of Grenada.

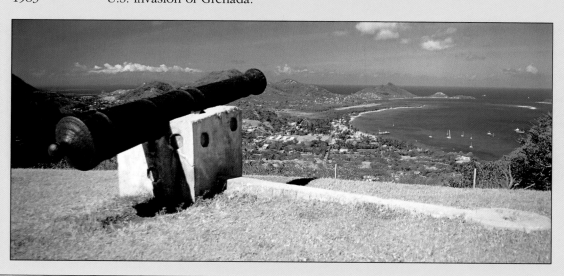

GOVERNMENT

GRENADA'S ROAD TO SELF-GOVERNMENT began at the turn of the 20th century. This period was characterized by racial prejudice, labor unrest, and the emergence of dominant political leaders.

The British ruled Grenada as a Crown Colony. The governor was the head of government, assisted by a legislative council of nominated members. In the 1920s some council members could be voted in by both colored and white residents who met strict property qualifications. These "unofficial" council members were expected to support any laws proposed by the governor.

To protect their interests, the professional classes and planters formed associations that had links to the government. The workers and farm laborers turned to organized labor movements. These grew in strength, led successful strikes, and eventually developed into political parties.

Left: **Prime Minister Herbert Blaize visiting British Prime Minister Margaret Thatcher at her office at No. 10, Downing Street.**

Opposite: **The calendar says it all: the revolutionist Maurice Bishop was a hero in the hearts of many Grenadians.**

FEDERATION FAILS

The movement toward self-government became stronger in the 1920s. It was often led by men who had served in the British West India regiment during World War I. One of the early leaders of Grenada was T. Albert Marryshow. He gathered a group of middle-class Grenadians of color who wanted a federation of Caribbean states to replace Crown Colony rule and formed the Representative Government Association in 1914.

Similar movements took place on most of the smaller British-ruled islands. All demanded to have some say in local government. Islanders wanted at least some members of their legislative assemblies to be elected from the local population. Many also supported a political union of the West Indies colonies. There was a short attempt at a federation of Grenada with nine other islands in 1958 but it failed. The federation dissolved, and Grenada became a British Associated State in 1967.

Opposite: **Herbert Blaize and his wife after he became prime minister of Grenada.**

WEST INDIES FEDERATION

On January 3, 1958, Grenada joined nine other Caribbean states to form the West Indies Federation. Its partners were Antigua and Barbuda, Barbados, Dominica, Jamaica, Montserrat, St. Kitts-Nevis-Anguilla, St. Lucia, Trinidad and Tobago, St. Vincent, and the Grenadines. The federation did not have full self-government because the governor-general was appointed by Great Britain. The governor-general appointed the members of the Council of State and had the right to veto bills. Members of the federal House of Representatives were elected, and they chose their prime minister. But the federation was short lived, surviving for only three years before conflict between its two largest states, Trinidad and Tobago, and Jamaica, killed it. Bauxite mining on Jamaica and oil exports from Trinidad boosted the economies of these two countries, and their leaders were afraid that the poorer islands would be a drain on their economies. Jamaica left the federation in 1961. It was quickly followed by Trinidad and Tobago. The federation was dissolved soon after. An attempt by Barbados to hold the remaining states together failed because the smaller islands were afraid of being dominated by Barbados.

UNIONS

Many unions emerged in the British colonies. Affiliated to British labor unions, these unions had the support of the British Labour Party.

Various political parties were formed during this period. Their common aim was to improve the lives of their people through education, social welfare, and better economic conditions. But achieving independence was the most important goal. Because their campaign platforms were similar, the success or failure of a party was often dependent on the charisma of its leaders.

One of the most controversial union leaders was Eric Matthew Gairy. An elementary school teacher, he rose to prominence when he organized a successful strike in 1951 that forced the British governor to negotiate. He became a leader in both the independence and labor movements. His Grenada United Labor Party (GULP) was strongly supported by peasants and farmers. In the 1962 election, however, he lost to the Grenada National Party, led by Herbert Blaize. Blaize had campaigned for unity with Trinidad and Tobago. But when Prime Minister Williams of Trinidad rejected the idea of any union, Gairy was returned to power in 1967.

Supporters of Herbert Blaize's New National Party at a campaign rally in 1990. This was Grenada's first election after the 1983 invasion.

ROAD TO SELF-GOVERNMENT

In 1940 Britain's ultimate goal was to help its colonies achieve self-government through universal suffrage. They began to free colonies in Asia, Africa, and the Middle East.

In Grenada every adult was allowed to vote for members of the legislative assembly, which later became the lower house of parliament. At first, elected members on the executive council were given the responsibility of heading a ministry. When most government ministers were elected members of the assembly, the executive council effectively became a proper governing cabinet of ministers responsible to parliament. This transition was achieved in all the Crown Colonies by 1956.

Self-government occurred when the leader of the party with the greatest number of elected members became the chief minister and took over as governor. Britain continued to be responsible for the island's foreign policy and defense. When these functions were given to the island government, full independence was attained.

BRITISH-STYLE GOVERNMENT

All the Crown Colonies adopted a British-style government. In Grenada the Queen of England is still the head of state, represented by a governor-general who is appointed to the office.

Real political power is held by the prime minister who is head of the government and leader of the party with the greatest number of seats in the lower house of parliament. He presides over a cabinet of ministers.

There are two houses of parliament—the lower house or the House of Representatives, which has 15 members elected to five-year terms; and the upper house or Senate, which has 13 members who are appointed by the governor-general. Seven of the senators are appointed on the advice of the prime minister, three on the advice of the leader of the official opposition, and three on the advice of the prime minister in consultation with organizations that the senators are selected to represent. The president of the Senate is selected from among the senators. All Grenadians over 18 years of age are eligible to vote.

The parliament building is situated in the capital, St. George's.

Before Maurice Bishop came to power, he was a London-educated lawyer.

REVOLUTION

When Grenada gained independence on February 7, 1974, Eric Gairy became the first prime minister. In 1979, while Gairy was overseas, a group of armed rebels overthrew him in a bloodless coup. Their leader, Maurice Bishop, became prime minister of the new People's Revolutionary Government. Bernard Coard, the deputy leader, became the minister of finance.

Bishop's early rule saw an improvement in the lives of Grenadians. But then he was influenced by Cuban president Fidel Castro and adopted a communist-style government. He suspended the constitution and invited Cuban advisers to Grenada. There was no longer any press freedom under his rule, and the prison was packed with political prisoners.

His communist alignments made the United States and other Caribbean nations uneasy. On the other hand, there was a struggle for power between Bishop and the more left-wing members of his party.

In October 1983 the hardliners mounted a military coup and put Bishop under house arrest. Thousands of Bishop's supporters gathered at Fort George to demand his release. The army opened fire on the crowd and killed about 40 people. Bishop and several of his friends and advisers were then taken out and executed. The government imposed a four-day curfew with orders to shoot on sight any one found on the streets without permission.

A meeting of the Organization of Eastern Caribbean States (OECS) was held, and it was agreed that American help should be sought.

SIX-DAY INVASION

On October 25, 1983, at the request of the governor-general, a combined force of the OECS and the United States invaded Grenada. In the fighting, 70 Cubans, 42 Americans, and 170 Grenadians died. The Americans quickly installed an interim government, restored the island's constitution, and elections were held in December 1985.

This election brought the New National Party to power. The NNP was a coalition of three political parties, with Herbert Blaize as its leader. It won 14 of the 15 seats. The alliance did not last very long, as the elected members soon resigned in protest against the manner in which certain issues were handled by the prime minister.

In January 1989, at a party convention, Blaize was deposed and his place taken by Keith Mitchell, general secretary of the party and minister of Communications and Works.

The U.S. Army unloading their weapons at the Point Salines Airport just before the invasion.

Mitchell's rule did not last long either. He was soon dismissed, and power once more returned to Blaize, who had formed a new party called The National Party. But Blaize's term in office was troubled by severe illness and other difficulties. Opposition members in parliament pressed for new elections, and Mitchell threatened to call a vote of no confidence in the government. There was unrest—civil servants were angry that salary increases that had been promised were not received, and unions and workers went on strike. Meanwhile, Blaize's health deteriorated, and he died just before elections were due to be called.

THE 1990 ELECTIONS

In March 1990 Grenadians went to the polls once more. This time they had five parties to choose from. The National Democratic Congress, led by Nicolas Brathwaite, won seven seats, one short of a majority. A new government was formed when the New Party leader Ben Jones allied his party with the National Democratic Congress. An elected member of the Grenada United Labor Party also defected and joined the New Democratic Congress. Thus bolstered, the NDC then formed the new government.

In the June 1995 elections the New National Party, headed by Keith Mitchell, won eight seats, the National Democratic Congress (now headed by George Brizan) won five, and the Grenada United Labour Party under leader Jerry Seales won two seats.

Although the next election was due to be held in October 2000, Prime Minister Keith Mitchell called snap elections in January 1999 when two members of his ruling New National Party crossed over and joined the opposition in November 1998. The New National Party asked voters to stay committed to the course set by the present government,

OPERATION URGENT FURY

Several conditions precipitated American and OECS (Organization of Eastern Caribbean States) action against Grenada. After the assassination of Maurice Bishop, the military council took control of the island, but there was utter chaos in the streets. The United States was also concerned that the Cuban-built Point Salines Airport would have a potential military use, and Grenada could become a missile base for the Cubans. The presence of some American medical students studying at St. George's Medical School provided the needed excuse, and the invasion was ordered on the strength of protecting these students from the unstable situation. On October 25, 1983, 21 helicopters from the aircraft carrier Guam landed on the beach near Pearls Airport on the eastern side of the island. There was token resistance and anti-aircraft fire, but this was quickly silenced. Another landing of helicopters farther south near the town of Grenville met with little resistance. Grenadians waved to the invading forces and welcomed them as liberators. By October 31 the Americans had gained complete control of the island, and the six-day war was over. Some members of the People's Revolutionary Government escaped, while most of them voluntarily surrendered.

Traffic police points such as the one below used to be a common sight in Grenada. Today most of them have been replaced by traffic lights.

while the opposition parties formed a coalition and advocated change. When the votes were counted, Mitchell's party won convincingly, winning all 15 seats in the House of Representatives.

KEEPING THE PEACE

Grenada's judicial system, like its government, is modeled after that of Britain. Grenada is a member of the Eastern Caribbean Supreme Court, which is composed of regional courts that are overseen by the Privy Council in England. An associate judge resides in Grenada.

Judges are appointed to the Supreme Court by a governmental body. The lower courts are under the control of magistrates who are also appointed. The crime rate in Grenada is low, and often the only matter that the courts deal with is that of petty theft.

Grenada has no army. Peace in the country is enforced by the Royal Grenada Police Force, which is led by a police commissioner. After the U.S. intervention in 1983, instructors from Britain and Barbados trained a new police force to ensure that there would be adequate security after the foreign troops departed.

GRENADA'S SIX PARISHES

For the purpose of local adminstration, the island of Grenada is divided into six parishes. Beginning with the parish of St. George in the southwest and moving clockwise, they are St. John, St. Mark, St. Patrick, St. Andrew, and St. David. St. George is home to 32,000 people and is where the capital and the port of St. George's is situated. It is the most urbanized and richest parish.

More than 8,000 people live in the parish of St. John. The main town is Gouyave, a major fishing area. The main attractions in St. John are the Belvidere and Dougaldston estates, where bananas, cocoa, nutmeg, and other spices are grown. There is a large nutmeg processing station where nutmegs and mace are prepared for shipment.

St. Mark is the smallest parish, with a population of just under 4,000 people. Fishing and agriculture are the major

industries. Grenada's highest peak, Mount St. Catherine, is located in this parish. St. Patrick in the north is an historic parish. It is where Amerindian petroglyphs have been found and where the Caribs leaped to their deaths in 1653 rather than surrender. Many old homes and plantation houses have been restored to their original beauty. St. Andrew is the largest producer of export crops—cocoa, nutmeg and bananas. The main town of Grenville holds a Rainbow City Festival every August, a celebration of the arts and crafts of the region. St. David is home to about 11,000 people and the last known habitat of the endangered Grenada Dove. La Sagesse Nature Centre offers visitors hiking trails through an old wooded estate and tours of a mangrove estuary.

ECONOMY

AGRICULTURE IS THE MOST IMPORTANT SECTOR of the Grenadian economy and employs the largest number of people. This has always been the case, from the time of the early French settlers who cultivated indigo and tobacco until the present day. Agriculture accounts for about 9.7% of the gross domestic product (GDP). The three most important crops are nutmeg, bananas, and cocoa, which were introduced to the country in the 18th century.

Tourism and manufacturing, however, are areas that the government is encouraging, and they are growing in importance. Tourism is a big earner of foreign exchange and accounts for more than 8% of the GDP. With its beautiful beaches, mountain scenery, and tropical climate, Grenada is a very attractive vacation spot for the growing number of tourists who arrive by air and sea.

Left: **A trading schooner brings agricultural produce to the markets in the bigger cities.**

Opposite: **As the economy improves, construction of new factories becomes increasingly important.**

Above: **A factory worker airing cocoa beans. Cocoa is grown lower down the hillsides in areas of medium rainfall, while nutmeg is grown in areas that receive the greatest rainfall.**

Opposite: **Spices are sorted by hand to eliminate any rotten ones.**

AGRICULTURE

Sugarcane was an important crop in Grenada in the 18th century. Power for crushing the sugarcane came from wind and water mills. When sugarcane lost its economic value, other crops were cultivated.

In 1714 agricultural production was diversified to include cocoa, coffee, and cotton. In 1782 Sir Joseph Banks, the botanical adviser to King George III, introduced nutmeg to Grenada. The island's soil was ideal for growing the spice, and because it was closer to Europe than the Dutch East Indies, Grenada became an important source of spices for European traders.

In the late 19th century, coconut and spices like cloves and cinnamon were grown. Breadfruit, avocados, and fruit trees such as papaya, mango, and five-finger fruit (or starfruit) were also grown. Bananas became an important cash crop after Hurricane Janet hit the island in 1955. Farmers could earn money quickly while they waited for their devastated crops to recover. This is because bananas can be harvested seven to nine months after planting.

SPICES

Grenada produces one-third of the world's supply of nutmeg. Nutmeg is an important ingredient in the flavoring of foods, drinks, sauces, and preserves. The tree is a tropical evergreen that can grow very tall, up to a height of 60 feet (18 m). It takes eight years for a nutmeg tree to fully mature, but fruit production increases each year. The fruit is round and yellow and appears all year, but the harvest is especially bountiful during the months of February to April and from August to October.

When the fruit is mature, it splits open to reveal a dark brown shell that contains the nutmeg. The shell is covered by a bright red, lacy membrane called mace. The mace is stripped from the shell and dried separately. It is a spice on its own and is also used by the pharmaceutical industry. Nutmeg and mace produce almost 40% of Grenada's revenue from export crops. Nutmeg is so important that it is an emblem on the country's flag. Indonesia is the world's only other large producer of nutmeg.

Grenada also produces many other spices—allspice (the dried berry of the pimento tree), bay leaves, hot and sweet peppers, cinnamon, cloves, ginger, and vanilla.

Fishermen pulling their nets out to sea. Smaller schools of fish such as jack, couvalli, and bonita are caught with seine nets near the shore.

FISHING

Fish is plentiful around the coral reefs that surround Grenada. Fishermen who take their boats out during the traditional "ocean season" from November to June bring in tuna, kingfish, flying fish, and dolphin. This accounts for about half of the year's catch. For the rest of the year, fishermen have a good time harvesting bottom-dwelling snapper, grouper, and other tropical rockfish.

Another kind of fishing involves catching shellfish, lobsters, turtles, and conch. White sea urchins are harvested for their eggs. The eggs are collected and put into clean sea urchin cases, then baked and sold.

The fishing industry has received a lot of foreign aid, particularly from Venezuela and Japan. This has made possible the construction of fish centers where the catch can be stored in cold rooms.

Most of the catch from Carriacou and Petit Martinique is sold to exporters. There are public fish markets in Grenada, but fishermen still sell their fish directly from their landing site.

TOURISM

Most tourists arrive on large cruise ships that dock at the pier in St. George's harbor, one of the most beautiful deep-water harbors in the Caribbean. Each year 300 cruise ships bring more than 250,000 visitors to the island. When passengers disembark, they find that they are immediately in the heart of St. George's, with all major attractions just a short distance away. A nearby vendors' market becomes a hive of activity on cruise ship day, with stalls set up to sell food, clothing, and souvenirs. About 100,000 more tourists arrive by air each year. Over 80 establishments, ranging from small budget guest houses to luxurious hotels with hundreds of rooms, provide accommodation.

A luxurious resort in Grenada.

Unloading grain from a cargo ship. Most imports come from the United Kingdom, the United States, and Trinidad and Tobago.

SMALL INDUSTRIES

In 1997 manufacturing made up 7% of the country's gross domestic product. The older industries are the garment and furniture making industries, food and fruit preserving and canning, rum distillation, small cottage industries, and cigarette production. These are still important in the country, but newer industries such as industrial gases, paints and varnishes, and flour and animal feeds, are being encouraged.

Besides nutmeg, cocoa, mace, bananas, and other fruit, Grenada's principal exports include vegetables, fish, flour, and clothing. Imports include food and live animals, beverages, fuel and lubricants, machinery, transport equipment, and other manufactured goods. The main trading partners are the other members of the Organization of Eastern Caribbean States (OECS): St. Vincent, Dominica, St. Lucia, and Antigua; members of the Caribbean Community (Caricom): Jamaica, Guyana, Barbados, Bahamas, and Trinidad; other Caribbean states; the European Community; and the United States.

OVER LAND AND SEA

The international airport at Point Salines in the south of the island is Grenada's connection with the rest of the world. It is linked by air to other Caribbean states by LIAT (Leeward Islands Air Transport), the region's main air carrier, and several other smaller airline companies that operate inter-island routes. The Airlines of Carriacou connects the island with the mainland of Grenada. There is a small airport at Lauriston on Carriacou.

On the sea there are ferries and shipping lines that operate regularly scheduled trips between the many harbors of Grenada, Carriacou, and Petit Martinique, and between Grenada and the other Caribbean islands.

The Grenadian transportation network is well developed, and most of the roads, including those on Carriacou and Petit Martinique, are paved, although extremely narrow, winding, and steep. The main road on Grenada circles the island, linking St. George's with all the coastal villages.

The international airport at Point Salines accommodates modern jumbo jets, receiving flights from cities in the United States, Canada, and Europe.

GRENADIANS

MORE THAN 80% OF ALL GRENADIANS are of African descent, while the remainder of the population consists of a small percentage of East Indians, Europeans, and other races.

When the Spanish first arrived in the Caribbean, they found three major groups of people, all of whom had come from South America. The Ciboney lived on the northwestern tip of Cuba and Hispaniola. The Bahamas, Greater Antilles, and Trinidad were dominated by the Arawaks, while the Caribs were found on the Virgin Islands, on many islands of the Lesser Antilles, and on the northwestern tip of Trinidad.

The Arawaks told the Spanish they had arrived on the islands after the Ciboney and then the Caribs had chased them away. There were no written records, so the Spanish accounts and archeological evidence are the only basis of truth for these assertions. But archeologists believe they are true.

To assume that Grenadians are only African is too narrow a view. Many of them have English, French, Dutch, Portuguese, Polish, Amerindian, or Chinese ancestors.

Left: **A vendor proudly holding up her handmade dolls.**

Opposite: **A Grenadian man selling steel drums in a tourist market near the Carenage.**

A Carib canoe exhibited at the National Museum.

INDIGENOUS PEOPLE

The Ciboneys were the most primitive group. They lived in rock shelters and caves by the coast, and survived by collecting shellfish, fruit, and herbs, and by hunting and fishing. They wore minimal clothing, painted their bodies, and used stone tools.

The Arawaks and Caribs had a more advanced way of life. Besides hunting and fishing, they cultivated the land, wore handwoven clothing, made pottery, lived in huts, and had boats. They used a sophisticated method of cultivation that required the burning off of forest and brush. They grew cassava, yams, sweet potatoes, and many other crops.

To supplement their diet, they hunted birds, iguanas, snakes, and small insects, and fished for a variety of marine life. They loved eating the eggs and flesh of the green turtle. Food was cooked by simmering ingredients in a pot. These eating habits have continued to this day— the green turtle is a delicacy, and the "one-pot" meal consisting of vegetables and meat is often eaten.

The Caribs were seafaring people and great boat builders. More war-like than the Arawaks, they had some success resisting the European powers. The Arawaks and the Caribs lived relatively healthy lives until the Europeans arrived, bringing new diseases with them. They were not immune to these diseases and fell ill. This, plus the hard labor that the Europeans forced them to perform, led to their extermination. When Columbus first arrived in the Caribbean in 1492, there were about 750,000 Amerindians. Within 20 years they were almost all dead.

SLAVERY

The Europeans imported slaves from the west coast of Africa to replace the labor that they had lost, especially on islands where sugar had been planted. The slave trade reached its peak in the 17th and 18th centuries. The Dutch, French, and British established settlements and warehouses along the west coast of Africa where slaves were held in preparation for their arduous journey across the Atlantic. Britain was the main slaving nation. Between 1690 and 1807, British traders brought over more than 2.5 million slaves to the Caribbean and Spanish America. Sometimes an entire shipload of slaves would be sold to one planter, but it was more common for them to be sold at a public auction. In this way families were broken up, and slaves coming from a single tribe were deliberately separated from each other. When all the less than able-bodied slaves had been sold, the healthy ones were often sold at a "scramble." The slaves were put in an enclosure and, at the sound of a bell, the buyers would rush in and scramble for whomever they could get.

Slaves who were shipped from West Africa were packed into ships like sardines in a tin. They watched as their companions fell ill, suffered, and died. Some threw themselves overboard in desperation.

PLANTATION LIFE

Life on the plantation was hard. A slave had to work extremely long hours and received poor food and little clothing. Many of them died of exhaustion or illness and were replaced by more slaves. By law, a Grenadian slave was entitled to a bit of land to grow provisions, or to receive "ground provisions" or root crops in the place of land, a house in which to live, a weekly ration of salt and salted fish, and an annual quota of clothing. However, more often than not, the slaves got nothing in return for their toil.

Many rebelled by running away to join Maroon communities in the undeveloped interior of the island, by malingering in the fields, or by

A farmer harvesting his fruit. Bananas became an important crop after the hurricane of 1955.

damaging the property of their masters. By the 1750s almost 90% of the people on sugar-growing islands were slaves. By the end of the 18th century, slaves had to do every kind of task conceivable—they were laborers, gang drivers, and overseers. In towns they could become skilled craftsmen. Their situation ranged from total bondage to comparative freedom.

The lives of the people, especially the slaves, improved dramatically when the plantation system disintegrated in the 1820s. Many religious and social organizations were formed to improve their lives, and most of them provided religious instruction to the slaves. These included the Society for the Education of the Poor, which started the Central School in St. George's for the children of the free blacks and colored, the Society for the Promotion of Christian Knowledge, and the Grenada District Committee. The clergy, all paid by the government, visited the estates and gave instruction to the slaves. It was at this time that many of them converted to Christianity.

After the slaves were freed, many worked on their own small plots of land or cultivated a shared area with other former slaves.

INDENTURED LABOR

After emancipation in 1834, planters relied on labor brought in from other countries. Indians, Portuguese, Maltese, and even Africans arrived on the island. The free Africans who came as indentured immigrants later joined their fellow tribespeople who had arrived before them in forming villages and cultivating the land.

Most of the Indians came from Calcutta and Madras. They saved up their money, and when many returned to India later, they brought home a sizeable amount of savings. Others emigrated to Trinidad and British Guyana. Many of them converted to Christianity from Hinduism and Islam.

Back from school, these children share their joy of being Grenadians with the photographer.

THE PEOPLE TODAY

Grenadians today are very much a product of their history. The experience of slavery has resulted in a tendency to reject authority and all its symbols, as well as a disdain for manual labor and for working in the hot sun. From the French and the English, the Grenadians gained religion and education, as well as a legal and political structure. The French influence today is limited to the names of people and places, and some expressions that have lingered in daily language. English has given Grenadians a means to gain access to global opportunities and become a part of the world at large.

Politically and economically, the United States plays an extremely important role in Grenadian life. Its proximity has made it easy for Grenadians to be exposed to American values and culture. In addition to roti, peas, and rice, Grenadians eat fast food, wear T-shirts and jeans, are attracted by brand named goods, and watch American television. Their sports idols are not just local cricket player Junior Murray but also American basketball star Michael Jordan.

Underlying this is their African heritage, evident in their speech and rhythmic movements. Grenadians also identify with the rest of the Caribbean world, which shares this very same mix of influences.

THE SISTER ISLANDS

While the people who live on Grenada's sister islands consider themselves to be a part of Grenada, they are proud of their special identities as "Kayaks" (as the Carriacouans call themselves) and Petit Martiniquans. The earliest settlers on Carriacou were French turtle hunters and fishermen. They were quickly joined by migrants from the neighboring French island of Guadeloupe who left their homes when their crops were destroyed by ants. As on the island of Grenada, the evidence of French occupation is clear in the names of villages on the island—Ma Chapelle, L'Esterre, Belair, and BelleVue. Sugar and cotton plantations were later developed, and hundreds of slaves were imported to help cultivate the crops. Carriacouans have a unique culture that is a blend of European—British, French, and Scottish—and African traditions. While much of the original culture has been diluted on other islands, the people of Carriacou have retained many of their traditions. This can be attributed to the fact that there were mainly absentee planters on the island. The slaves were therefore less restricted and able to retain more of their traditions than those on Grenada. This is seen in the survival of the Big Drum ceremony, folk beliefs and dances, and special celebrations such as the Boat Launching ceremony, Carnival, and Parang festivals.

Petit Martinique, like Carriacou, was settled by the French. The people of Petit Martinique have always been known for their proud and independent lifestyle, which is intimately linked to the sea. The men are either fishermen or sailors, while the women tend the crops and are used to fending for themselves and their children during the long absences of their menfolk. Petit Martinique has a reputation for being a smuggler's paradise. This was probably because the independent lifestyle and ability to sail to other ports led them to smuggling as a simple way of obtaining items that they needed.

LIFESTYLE

WITH BALMY TROPICAL WINDS, warm temperatures, and a relaxed attitude, life on Grenada moves to a slower rhythm than that of the United States. Visitors to the island quickly succumb to this leisurely pace, and much has been said about the Caribbean islander's lack of a sense of time.

Villages are strung out along the main island highway: houses clinging to the hillsides and congregating where there is sufficient space to form little communities. There is at least one church, a school or two, the village green where local soccer matches are played, and numerous corner drink and grocery shops.

The church is an important anchor in Grenadian life. All life events—a birth in the family, marriage, and death—are celebrated there. However, as in many other parts of the world, the old traditions have less influence on people today.

Left: **Unloading supplies from a boat. It is sometimes necessary for villagers living on the smaller islands to buy groceries from the larger Grenada Island.**

Opposite: **A man taking a rest before proceeding to the market to sell his produce.**

VILLAGE RHYTHMS

Grenada's villages are mainly fishing and farming communities where life is not ruled by the clock. Fishermen put their boats out in the morning and come back at the end of the day with their catch. They blow on a conch shell to announce that they have fish to sell. When a fishing boat comes in, everyone, especially the children, goes down to the beach, curious to see what the catch is.

Houses are usually simple and rectangular in shape, with two or three bedrooms, a living area, a kitchen, and a bathroom. If more space is required, a wooden shed may be added to the side. Bushes with colorful leaves and flowers are often planted in the front and serve to divide one yard from another. Vegetable gardens flourish behind the houses together with many fruit trees. A family may own a few goats and cows tethered to a nearby tree or post, and some chickens. If they have a small plot of land to farm, whole families will be engaged in agriculture. Families with less money live in wooden houses.

Vegetables, spices, and fruit can all be found in a market.

MARKET DAY

Markets are integral to a Grenadian's life. Women cultivate vegetables for their families and take the excess to the market to sell. The market functions most of the week except Sunday, from early morning to late afternoon. It is most lively on Saturdays. The largest Saturday markets are in the towns of St. George's and Grenville.

Stalls are often nothing more than makeshift boxes of scrap wood nailed together, topped off with large and colorful umbrellas. People gather not only to shop for the items they need but also to spend time chatting with their friends. The streets are filled with groups of men and women "liming," as a Grenadian might say, meaning just standing around and relaxing with friends.

Meat and fish are sold at specialized markets such as the Melville Street Fish Market and Abattoir on Grenada Island. Women sell mainly small fish called jacks from wooden trays set upon pails full of fish. A carved-up green turtle is occasionally part of the morning's offering.

Vegetables, spices, and fruit can all be found in a market.

Above: **A street in St. George's.**

Opposite: **A female worker in a spice factory.**

TRANSPORTATION

The family car is often a small sedan, but pickups and four-wheel drive vehicles are fairly common. Bicycles and motorbikes are commonly seen on weekends, when young boys whizz down the streets on their way to the beach. Those without their own means of transportation walk wherever they can. For longer journeys, a taxi or bus is indispensable.

Taxis are costly and are preferred by tourists. Most Grenadians use buses, which are minivans that carry up to 18 passengers comfortably. The bus is operated by a driver and his assistant who try to get as many people in the bus as they can to maximize the revenue from each trip. Buses crammed with passengers are a common sight. As Grenada's roads are narrow and winding, a bus ride can often be a hair-raising experience.

Bus terminals are in the heart of St. George's near the Market Square and the Esplanade, and bus routes fan out from there to cover the entire island. While there are bus stops, buses will pick up passengers anywhere along the route, even though it is illegal to do so.

GRENADIAN WOMEN

Women have always been a source of cheap unskilled and semiskilled labor in Grenada. During the days of slavery, they were field and house slaves. After emancipation, they became laborers on plantations. They later worked in factories. Even if they did not work outside the home, they planted gardens and sold their extra provisions in the market to earn money.

Women are still employed in traditional female occupations today. Many of them are in domestic service or work as seamstresses, hairdressers, and factory workers. The more educated are often teachers and nurses and work in the service sector, such as tourism. Some hold administrative and senior management positions in private companies, the public service, and political office, but they are small in number.

Grenadian women have always had the major responsibility for caring and nurturing the family, even when the male head of household is present. Many have to work to help supplement the family income. Having their own money gives them a sense of independence, self-esteem, and power in their family and community.

65

THE FAMILY UNIT

Grenadians tend to be traditional and conservative in their outlook. The family unit is important, and the concept of family goes beyond immediate members to embrace extended members, close friends, and neighbors.

Most women are expected to bear children and to be responsible for their care and upbringing. Women tend to bear children at an early age. In the late 1990s the average Grenadian woman gave birth to three or four children. Teenage pregnancies are not uncommon and often result in the young woman having to leave school prematurely. Women who have no children of their own often care for the children of others. Therefore, besides their mothers, children may be raised by their other close relatives, friends, or neighbors.

In return, the children are expected to look after their parents in their old age. Parents look forward to their children "doing well" and being able to financially support them. The values of respect for elders and sharing in the family are instilled in children when they are very young.

A TRADITIONAL GRENADIAN WEDDING

Weddings are spectacular affairs that involve ceremonies such as the dancing of the cake and dancing the flag. The bride's and groom's wedding cakes are displayed by selected women from each side of the family who "dance the cake" on trays. In the same way, male dancers from both sides dance with the groom's and the bride's flags. This is a light-hearted but thrilling competition in which each dancer tries to gain supremacy, but it is finally the groom's cake and flag that must always be kept above the bride's, because he is the head of the family.

After the competition, both flags are placed above the bride's home. The wedding reception may be held at the bride's home or in a hall if the crowd is too large. A procession of cars, all tooting their horns, announces the arrival of the wedding couple, and the guests file out to greet them and shower them with rice. They enter the home passing under an archway of coconut palms and accompanied by a string band. Inside, the wedding couple is greeted by their parents and led to the wedding table for a reception. There is lots of music and dancing. Once it ends, the couple pack their things into a car and drive to their new home.

RITUALS OF DEATH

The rituals that accompany a death incorporate both Christian practices and folk beliefs. The family of the deceased is responsible for the funeral preparations. During the wake, the men and boys will build the coffin in one corner of the yard, while the women and girls prepare mourning clothes, headcloths, and ribbons for the mourners. Food is prepared—usually tea with bread or biscuits, and rum. A spicy tea made from the leaves of the bunden bush was traditionally served, but coffee is a modern substitute.

On the day of the burial, the coffin is borne to church or to the cemetery. Hymns are sung along the way. Two chairs are taken along to place the coffin on if a change of bearers is required. At the entrance to the cemetery, the chairs are turned upside down to allow the spirit of the dead to leave the chairs. When bearers are relieved of their burden, they shake out their arms to transfer the spirit back to the coffin.

An evergreen tree is planted to mark the tomb. Relatives who visit after the funeral throw water and rum on it. A prayer meeting is also held after the funeral at the house where the death occurred. On that day a *saraca* ("SAH-ra-ca") or special sacrificial feast is prepared.

A tombstone for the grave is not erected until enough time has passed to allow the earth to settle. The placing of the stone requires a "stone feast." The stone is first placed on the main bed in the house, and a sacrificial plate of food is placed on a table. The stone is then taken outside where it is blessed with a sprinkling of water, rum, rice, and eggs. Prayers are said before it is ceremoniously taken to the cemetery and placed on the grave. Then a Big Drum ceremony is held, followed by much feasting and dancing. The food is cooked in big pots and includes stewed peas, ground provisions (root vegetables), bananas, rolled rice, *coo coo* (ground corn meal cooked into a cake with coconut, salt, and water), and plenty of meat—pork, chicken, and mutton.

BIRTH

Less ceremony is involved when there is a birth in the family. With improved medical services, most women now have their babies delivered in the maternity ward of a hospital, under the care of doctors and nurses.

When births at home were more the norm, especially in the villages, the delivery was taken care of by the district nurse or doctor. The father did not involve himself in the event but remained outside the room until he was called. If a birth was difficult, the woman's parents would walk around the house pouring rum and water at each corner and praying for a safe and quick delivery. The umbilical cord and afterbirth was often buried under a tree. After giving birth the mother was not allowed to go outdoors but had to remain in the house for eight days. Tradition dictates that she has to bathe twice a day. When friends and relatives visit the family, they bring food and gifts for the mother and a silver coin for the newborn baby.

The Grenadian government set up Cedars Women's Shelter for abused women and children in 1999. This center provides temporary shelter and counseling for women and children in need of help.

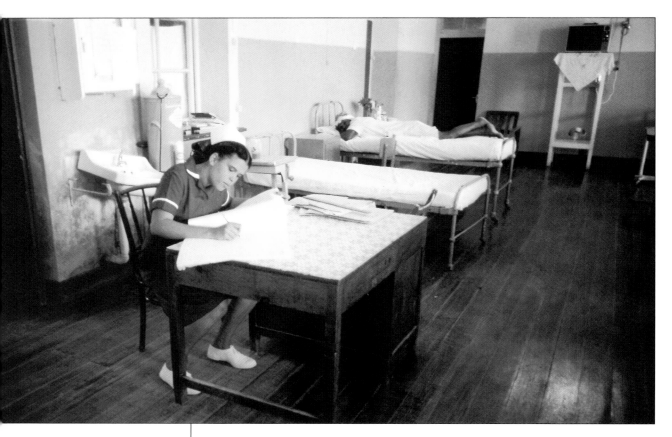

HEALTH

There are three hospitals in Grenada. The main one is the General Hospital in St. George's. The other two are in the parish of St. Andrew and on Carriacou. These hospitals are able to take care of most medical problems, but serious cases may be sent to the larger Caribbean island of Barbados or to the United States.

Health centers and district medical stations provide essential healthcare services for the rest of the rural areas. There are also homes for handicapped children and the elderly. Grenadians do not have to pay for their medical and dental treatment, which is provided by the government.

Life expectancy has improved dramatically over the last half a century as a result of better healthcare and a higher standard of living. Today most Grenadians expect to live into their 70s.

EDUCATION

Grenada has inherited the British system of education. Education is free and compulsory for children from 5 to 16 years of age. At the end of primary school, children take a common entrance examination. If they pass and are under the age of 16, they can continue their education in a secondary school. If they are over 16, they pursue a technical education.

Secondary school is five years during which students prepare for an examination set by the Caribbean Examination Council, after which they may move on to a pre-university level of studies at the Grenada National College. At the end of two years, they take an "A" level examination set by the Cambridge Board of Education in the United Kingdom. Except for a few private ones, most schools are coeducational.

Young Grenadians can also choose to enter the Technical and Vocations Institute to study agriculture, secretarial skills, drafting, auto mechanics, plumbing, and other courses. St. George's University is the highest institution of learning in Grenada. It began as a school of medicine in 1977 but has since expanded to include arts and sciences and a school of graduate studies. Students can attend a branch of the University of the West Indies in Grenada.

RELIGION

WHEN THE EUROPEANS FIRST ARRIVED in the Caribbean, they thought that the indigenous people whom they encountered—the Arawaks and the Caribs—had no religion. Although they did not have a religion recognizable to the Europeans, they did have beliefs that were of a religious or supernatural nature.

The indigenous people were animists, believing in the existence of many spirits that could interfere with or influence human life. These spirits were associated with natural elements or phenomena that they controlled. They could inhabit physical objects, which the natives worshipped, and people could be possessed by spirits. When this happened, the spirit had to be exorcized by a priest or shaman.

Even when young, these people had a clear sense of what it meant to be good or bad. For the Caribs, it was good to be courageous and resourceful in battle, for they were a warlike people. Good behavior for the Arawaks, on the other hand, was to be gentle and peace-loving.

The Europeans tried to convert them to the Christian faith. For much of the Greater Antilles, the conquering and "civilizing" of the indigenous people was done by the Spanish. In Grenada, as in many other islands of the Lesser Antilles, the task was undertaken by the French colonizers. However, hostilities between the French colonizers and the Caribs broke out, leading finally to the expulsion and extermination of all Carib people on the island of Grenada.

Above: **St. Andrew's Presbyterian Church, or Scots' Kirk, was built in 1831. It is well known for its bell and clock. The church bell was cast in Glasgow.**

Opposite: **A Baptist at a prayer meeting.**

ARRIVAL OF THE DOMINICANS

With the French colonial government came the establishment of the Roman Catholic religion. The first Roman Catholic mission to arrive in Grenada was the Dominican order. The Dominicans were given land to help establish them in their missionary work. They were followed by the Capuchins who, in 1690, built a church in Fort Royal, then another one in the capital. An Anglican church now stands on that site.

When Grenada was ceded to the British in 1763, the British government established the Church of England (or the Anglican Church) on the island. This led to the persecution of the Roman Catholic Church from 1783 to 1795. Roman Catholic relics, altars, and baptismal fonts were destroyed. The settlers on Grenada, who were mainly French, were pressured to give up their Roman Catholic faith and embrace Anglicanism. Many fled to Trinidad to escape the persecution, taking their slaves with them.

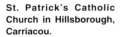

St. Patrick's Catholic Church in Hillsborough, Carriacou.

FOUR MAIN CHRISTIAN CHURCHES

By the 1800s there were four main denominations active in Grenada—the Anglicans, Roman Catholics, Methodists, and Presbyterians, or Church of Scotland. These churches competed for converts. The Anglican Church had the support of the colonial government and was a rich landowner. Together with the Church of Scotland, it attracted the ruling class and the planters. The Roman Catholic Church had the greatest number of followers who were mainly of the working class.

The churches brought with them missionaries who set up some of the first schools in the Caribbean. The first convent and school to be founded in Grenada was St. Joseph's Convent, established in 1876 by four nuns from Trinidad who belonged to the missionary order of St. Joseph of Cluny. The Sisters of St. Joseph of Cluny also opened another school in Grenville in 1953 and run a third school in the parish of St. David.

Today the antagonism between the faiths has been overtaken by a spirit of unity in which the various Christian churches live and work together.

St. George's Anglican Church was rebuilt by the British on the site of an earlier Roman Catholic church of 1690 built by the Capuchins. The Capuchin church was taken over by the Anglicans in 1784 and rebuilt in Georgian architecture in 1825 after an earthquake that year almost destroyed it. A clock installed in 1904 keeps the island's official time.

Above: **Traditionally, parents did not call their children by their real names but by false ones in order to mislead the spirits who might want to harm them.**

Opposite: **A Rastafarian. Rastafarians call one another "brother."**

TRADITIONAL BELIEFS

The slaves brought with them their African beliefs, but these practices were discouraged by the plantation owners and often banned. As a result many African religious practices soon died. Missionaries converted the slaves to Christianity. Today the church forms an integral part of village social life.

Most islanders belong to one Christian faith or another. More than 50% are Roman Catholics, 14% are Anglicans, and another 33% belong to other Protestant churches. A small segment of Grenadian society belongs to other faiths. The East Indians who came to Grenada brought their own beliefs with them. Most of them were Hindu, while a small percentage were Muslims. Many were converted to Christianity. There is no Hindu temple in Grenada, but there is a mosque at the southern end of the island.

Shango is an African religion that has limited influence in Grenada. Most followers of Shango also consider themselves Christians. Many of the African spirits or deities have their counterparts in the Christian saints or the Old Testament prophets. For example, Shango is identified with St. John, and Legba with the devil. Shango is the name of a spirit, a fierce preacher and a hunter.

Obeah, a kind of witchcraft or sorcery, is another African practice that has survived. A believer in obeah might go to an obeah practitioner to get him or her to cast a spell on an enemy.

Grenadians also believe that supernatural phenomena in this world can interfere with one's life. Children are especially vulnerable to interference by spirits and have to be protected.

RASTAS

Rastafarianism, a movement that began in Jamaica in the 1930s, has spread widely throughout the Caribbean, including Grenada. Rastafarians believe that the former Emperor of Ethiopia, Haile Selassie, is God, and that his crowning was the fulfilment of a prophecy: one day someone who would unite all Africans in one nation would rise up in Africa. They interpret the Bible in the light of their beliefs. They do not marry, but are faithful to their partners. The Rastafarians frown upon infidelity and promiscuity. Some Rastafarians grow their beards, sport dreadlocks, and wear robes.

LANGUAGE

ALMOST EVERYONE IN GRENADA SPEAKS ENGLISH. It is the official language of the country and is the language of instruction in schools. When African slaves were brought over to work on the plantations, they brought with them their own African languages. But laborer, overseer, and plantation owner all had to learn to understand each other and to communicate well. This was achieved through a natural process of creolization of the language

When Grenada was French, the people spoke a Creole that was a mixture of French and African dialect, but when the British took over control of the country, Grenadians changed to a Creole that was based on English. Today Creole French is hardly ever spoken except by some older people.

Left and opposite: **English is the most commonly used language in Grenada, whether in political slogans or on the signs of local stores.**

Grenadians use Creole English in the market-place.

CREOLE ENGLISH

There was a tendency in the past for people of the upper classes to speak Standard English and for those of the lower classes to speak a creolized dialect. This has resulted in a lingering "colonial" attitude towards language, including a class prejudice attached to speaking "bad English." It was a badge of good breeding and social class to speak "Queen's English" or "BBC English" (that spoken by a British Broadcasting Corporation announcer), and to acquire such an English accent was highly desirable.

Grenadian educator Clyde Belfon, who has made a study of the language of his people, believes that Creole English rather than Standard English (the English that Grenadians learn in school) is the first language of the people. It has its own syntax, vocabulary, song, and meaning.

This is, however, seldom admitted as there is a stigma associated with Creole English—many believe that it is "bad English," the language of uneducated people.

SOME COMMON EXPRESSIONS:

Just now—Don't expect something immediately.
Now for now—Right away.
Don't make me vex—Don't make me angry.
Don't mamaguey me—Don't tell me a lie.
Comess—A total confusion.
Fete—A party.
For so—For no reason.
Fete for so—A party on the spur of the moment.
Like bush, like peas—There is a lot of whatever it is.
Fete as bush—A grand party with plenty to eat and drink
Brango—Spicy gossip.
Play lougarou—To play the fool.
Sea bath—A swim.
Lime—Relax, hang around.
Beating mouth—To chat.
Farse—To be nosey.
Fire one—Drink rum.
Me tell you—I'm telling you.
You too sut—You are too stupid.
Make a blow—Buy a drink.
Study your head—Be careful what you say or do.
Pork ah pork no beef—Not of the best.
Don't give me a six for nine—Don't mislead me.
The firm big—The family has money.
Watch your case—Be careful.
Wood have ears—Someone may be listening.

Those who believe in the value of Creole English hope that the biased "colonial" attitude is dying, and that Creole English as it is spoken in Grenada, and shared with many other parts of the Caribbean, will eventually be recognized as a language in its own right.

Grenadians at a carnival.

THE FRENCH CONNECTION

Many place names in Grenada are French, such as Gouyave (Guava), Grand Etang (Great Lake), and L'Anse aux Epines (Beach of Pines). Many words come from French and Creole French. The first day of Carnival is called *jouvert* ("jou-vay") from *jour ouvert*, meaning "the beginning of day." Lajabless, the she-devil that storytellers frighten little children with, comes from *la diablesse*, meaning "female devil."

There are also expressions derived from French. "Well yes, oui!" is often used to express exasperation or indignation. *Bunjay*, from the expression *bon dieu*, is an exclamation of surprise or used for emphasis.

One good way to get a feel for Creole English is to read a novel such as *Tidal Wave*. The book is written by Clyde Belfon in both Standard English and Creole English. Another book is *Snowflakes in the Sun* by Grenadian writer Jean Buffong. It is filled with the special expressions of informal Grenadian English.

THE MEDIA

About 98% of Grenadians over the age of 15 can read and write. With such a high literacy rate, it is no wonder that the media have a long history. An entry in the 1946 *Grenada Handbook and Directory* claimed that the *Grenadian Chronicle*, which began publication in 1784, was "the oldest newspaper in the Western Hemisphere and the second oldest in the English-speaking world," having been established even before the *Times* of London, which began publication in 1788.

In 1915 the *Chronicle* ceased publication, giving way that year to a new newspaper, *The West Indian*. This paper later became a government paper. When the revolution took place in 1979, it was taken over by the revolutionary government and renamed the *Free West Indian*.

The major newspaper at the moment, the *Grenadian Voice*, was started in 1981 to give people an independent alternative to the *Free West Indian*. The *Grenadian Voice* is published weekly. There are two other independent weekly newspapers, the *Informer* and *Grenada Today*.

Radio Grenada is the island's only radio station and is state-owned. The island's first television station was built by the Cubans when the People's Revolutionary Government was in power, but it was destroyed during the invasion. A new station was built in 1985 with American aid. Grenada Television is owned by the government. It shows local news, sports, and entertainment. Cable television brings major U.S. network broadcasts to the island.

Grenadians are widely exposed to foreign music through the media.

ARTS

THE MUSIC OF THE CARIBBEAN—whether calypso, reggae, or soca—can be heard everywhere: on the radio, as you walk down the streets of Grenada, or from the back of a taxi or a bus. Much of the music has its roots in African folk music with drumming and strong rhythms.

Grenadians are a musical people, and this is seen in their love for dance. Many of the dances have African origins, but the French and English also contributed to the dance heritage of Grenada.

The arts scene is thriving, with folk artists, craftspeople, and storytellers. The modern version of the storyteller is found in the theater, or in the oral poetry performed in front of large crowds.

Even the houses on the island are a canvas for artistic expression. Their extremely colorful exteriors display the exuberance and gaiety that people bring to self-expression.

Left: **The National Museum in Carriacou.**

Opposite: **A steel drum band getting ready to perform.**

CALYPSO

Calypso had its beginnings in Trinidad in the 18th century—from there, it spread to the rest of the region. Calypso came about when slaves working on the plantations started to sing satirical songs in French patois. It was their way of mocking their European masters and expressing their discontent. In other songs, singers would try to outdo each other in a battle of words and verbal insults. The lyrics of early calypso songs were often composed on the spot, showing the creativity and wit of the singers.

Today calypso is usually sung in English, and many musicians continue to compose and perform it. The songs are still satirical and biting in their commentary on social and political conditions, exposing sham, pretence, and injustices in the Grenadian islands. There are often sexual innuendoes in the songs. The melody and the rhythms are similar, but the lyrics change from song to song.

Calypso competitions are an important part of Carnival celebrations, when many singers vie for the title of Calypso King. The singers like to take on special expressive names such as Atilla the Hun, King Pharoah, Lord Executor, and Duke of Iron.

FAMOUS CALYPSO SINGERS

One famous calypso singer is Slinger Francisco, better known as the Mighty Sparrow, or simply, Sparrow. Born in Grenada in 1935, Sparrow moved to Trinidad with his family when he was still a boy. The talented musician composed songs at an early age. His first public performance was in 1954, when he was only 19 years old. Two years later, he won the Trinidad Carnival calypso competition with his song, *Jean and Dinah*. He has since composed innumerable songs and has produced more than 40 music albums.

Sparrow has inspired many Grenadians who need little incentive to express the musical rhythm and creativity that seem to live in their souls. William Elcock, alias Scaramouche, is one such individual. From a large family of 12 children, Scaramouche lived in a house made of cane straw with a leaky roof when he was young. He ran away from his family by stowing away on board a boat bound for Trinidad. In Trinidad he hung around a steel band pan yard and found acceptance and a job as a general helper. Young William soon learned to play pan and became a professional player, performing with a steel band group. He also began to compose songs, eventually winning a calypso crown for one of his compositions. He joined the Mighty Sparrow and chose Scaramouche as his stage name because the film of that same title, starring Stewart Granger, was showing at the time.

After a short sojourn in America, Scaramouche returned to Grenada in 1970 and won the calypso crown that year. When Ronald Reagan, then President of the United States, visited Grenada in 1983, Scaramouche was chosen to sing for him. In 1994 he was again picked to entertain Princess Anne of Great Britain when she was visiting the nearby Grenadine island of Mustique.

Another influential singer in Grenada is Irie Francis, who has been singing calypso for more than 20 years. Francis is better known as the Mighty Arrow. He first learned to play the ukelele, then the guitar, and after that the pan or steel drum. Mighty Arrow's trademark technique is his ability to improvise songs for the people he meets. He believes the ability to improvise the songs is a gift, and that the lyrics just "come to him." Mighty Arrow performs at many hotel restaurants in Grenada's tourist belt, often accompanying himself on the guitar. When he is not performing, he tends his land in Requin in the parish of St. David.

Opposite: **A calypso singer entertaining tourists with his guitar.**

A steel drum souvenir. The different sections of a steel drum are made with such fine precision that each section will produce a different and desired note.

MUSICAL INSTRUMENTS

The most distinctive musical instrument in Grenada is the pan. Like calypso, the pan originated in Trinidad and is an instrument born out of ingenuity and creativity. People were determined to make music even when the colonial authorities banned their traditional percussion instruments. They found that the tops of discarded oil drums, which they retrieved from the garbage, could be coaxed into making music by specially "tuning" or beating them into shape.

The pan is the basic instrument of the steel band and is made from an oil drum with the bottom removed. The depth of the pan determines the pitch. After the bottom of the drum has been removed, the top is beaten into a concave shape that is divided into a number of sections separated by grooves that are chiseled into the concave surface. Each section is then beaten from the inside of the drum so that its surface is raised.

There are several types of pan—the ping pong or soprano pan, the second or alto pan, the third or tenor pan, and the bass pan. Each pan is able to play the notes of the musical scale, and a good steel band can play a wide range of popular and classical music.

FOLK DANCES

Many of the Grenadian folk dances originated with the African slavery, such as the *bongo* ("BON-goh") and the *kalinda* ("KA-lihn-dah"). Both dances were performed at wakes in the belief that they helped the dead

person transit from this world to the next. While the *bongo* has graceful movements, the *kalinda* resembles a choreographed stick fight.

The French and English also contributed to the dance heritage of Grenada. The Quadrille, a French dance popular in 18th century England, was introduced to Grenada by the English. The Quadrille was accompanied by the tambourine, bass drum, violin, and a triangle. At the end of the dance, it was the tradition to throw a bouquet so that the next Quadrille would be held in the home of the person who caught it. Another French dance that arrived in Grenada via England was the Lancers. It was performed by men dressed in tailcoats and frilled neck-pieces and women in long flowing gowns.

The Africans developed their own Belle Air, a dance that was inspired by the Quadrille and Lancers. They performed this barefoot and with equal grace and skill, but added color to the event. The women often wore bright headscarves with long-sleeved dresses and lacy petticoats, while the men had on headbands, colorful shirts, and white trousers or dungarees.

WARM CLIMATE, VIBRANT COLORS

The Grenadian hillside is covered with small, square houses that have been built on pier foundations. As there is no need to insulate against the cold, the outdoors is "brought" into the interior living environment in the form of verandas, porches, balconies, and large windows with louvered shutters. At first, houses retained their natural hues, but when paint became readily available, islanders expressed their creativity in their colorful houses.

There are no basements in the houses. A series of steps usually leads the visitor up to the main door. The houses are single or double-storied, and there are no high-rise buildings. Grenada prides itself on the fact that no building is allowed to be taller than a coconut palm.

There are many interesting historical buildings with distinctly European, especially French and English, architecture. The wrought-iron work along the Esplanade and Market Square in St. George's is an example of French influence. The British influence is seen in the Georgian-style buildings.

FOLK ARTISTS

The history of art is relatively young in Grenada. In the 20th century many Grenadians took up painting, drawing, and sculpting. Most artists were self-taught painters who used watercolors and oils. Instead of canvas, which is not easily available on the island, hard board or masonite was used as a painting surface. Their paintings include scenes of island life, blue skies, clear waters, fishermen and their nets, village life, market bustle, and children at play.

Grenadian artists are supported by the Grenada Arts Council, which organizes annual art shows. These shows provide many young artists an opportunity to exhibit their work outside of catering to the tourist's need for souvenirs. Two aspiring artists are Leslie Philip and Freddy Paul. A Carriacouan with a hearing disability, Philip works from home and paints in oils. Paul is a watercolorist who has dreams of developing an art gallery. Both are in their 20s and have won several awards for their work.

GRENADIAN HANDICRAFTS

Grenadian handicrafts have a long history, beginning with the early settlers who arrived from South America. Excavations at Point Salines in the south of Grenada, and Duquesne Bay and Sauteurs in the north, have unearthed finely crafted terracotta cooking pots and ceremonial vessels, intricate sculpture, arrowheads, and stone carvings.

Today many craftspeople make batik material, weave straw, bamboo, and wicker into hats, bags, and purses, carve furniture, kitchen utensils, and other useful and decorative household items out of mahogany, red cedar, and other woods, as well as make articles out of coral and turtle shell.

The villagers of Marquis, on the eastern side of Grenada Island, are known as expert weavers who are able to fashion all kinds of useful objects out of wild palm leaves.

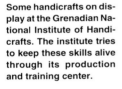

Some handicrafts on display at the Grenadian National Institute of Handicrafts. The institute tries to keep these skills alive through its production and training center.

THEATER AND LITERATURE

Grenadian theater began mainly as Shakespearean theater, a result of the English colonial period. Shakespearean plays were performed annually and on special occasions for the entertainment of the people. Many Grenadian actors got their start during this period. At the same time, there was theater based on folklore. The father of Grenadian folklore is Crofton McGuire of River Sallee, Grenada. A great storyteller and actor, he established the River Sallee Glee Club, which performs one-act plays and folk songs.

In the 1960s and 1970s Grenadian playwrights became more inward-looking and began to produce West Indian plays. Wilfred Redhead is an author from this period whose plays have been published and performed all over the Caribbean. His book, *A City on a Hill*, is a memoir of early St. George's. Writers also searched for a cultural identity, and oral poets performed in front of large crowds.

The national library on the Carenagh. The red-bricked building was formerly a warehouse. Today it is well used by school children who go there after school to do their research and homework.

Grenadian writer Omiwale David Franklyn has three books to his name. His latest book, *Bridging the Two Grenadas*, looks at the formation and transformation of Grenadian society and in particular the influence of two former prime ministers, Eric Gairy and Maurice Bishop, on these developments.

Another famous author is Merle Collins, who used to be a teacher and researcher in Grenada, a member of the National Women's Organization in Grenada, and a member of African Dawn, a group that performs poetry to African music. She has published several books, including a collection of poetry entitled *Because the Dawn Breaks*.

LEISURE

THE BRITISH NOT ONLY LEFT GRENADIANS A LEGACY in the system of government, the courts, and education, they also shared with them their love of soccer and cricket. Other leisure activities revolve around water, which is not surprising since Grenada is surrounded by water, and the climate in Grenada is tropical.

Grenadians love to have picnics by the sea or by waterfalls and to hike through the beautiful mountain ranges in the center of the island. Hunting is also popular.

Simple pleasures such as circle games continue to be passed down from generation to generation. Modern pastimes like watching television have also pervaded the Grenadian lifestyle. With the growth of tourism, nightclubs are also part of island life, and many local residents now prefer to dance the night away.

Left: **Boys taking a dip in the Carenage on a hot afternoon. Many of them like to swim in between the boats.**

Opposite: **A young, aspiring musician with his homemade guitar.**

95

CRICKET

Cricket was introduced to the English-speaking Caribbean region by the British, and Grenadians are excellent players. Cricket is played on an open green with two teams of 11 players each. The teams, whose players traditionally wear predominantly white uniforms, take turns trying to bat the ball and hit the wicket of the opposing team.

Unfortunately, having small populations, individual island nations have difficulty producing enough excellent players to form national teams that can compete internationally. Instead, Grenadian cricketers vie with others from among the various English-speaking Caribbean countries in competitions to select the best players to represent the West Indies in international championship games. Excitement runs particularly high when the West Indies is playing against England.

Grenada's best cricket player is Junior Murray. He made sporting history when he became the first Grenadian to represent the West Indies in an international championship game.

SOCCER

English football or soccer is another popular sport in Grenada. The Grenada Football Association has 28 member clubs that compete each year in the premier league. English football is is played by two teams of 11 players each. A game lasts for 90 minutes, and the objective is for the teams to score as many goals as possible.

The most successful football club is probably the Courts Hurricanes. It has won the Grenada National Championship more often than any other club. Between 1969 and 1976 it won the championship eight times consecutively. Steve Mark, a Hurricane, is one of Grenada's outstanding football players. He was named Caribbean Footballer of the Year in 1989 and plays professionally for teams in Chile and Barbados.

Every boys' school has cricket and football teams, and it is common to see young boys after school kicking a ball around on any available open ground. The Grenadian government is improving sports facilities and building a prestigious National Stadium at a cost of US$23 million. When completed, it will be the site for all major football and cricket games on the island.

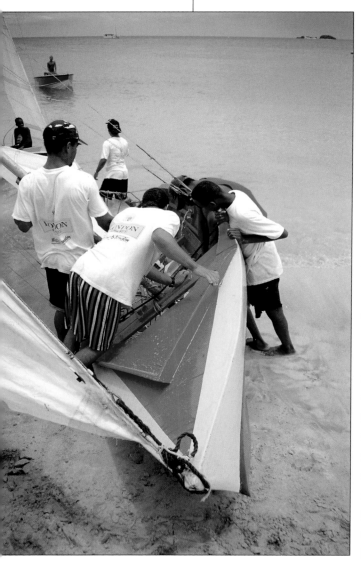

WATER SPORTS

Every Easter the Grenada Yacht Club holds a regatta where the main attraction is a race from Trinidad to Grenada. The Carriacou Regatta, which is held around late July or early August, is a much bigger affair. It usually takes place on a weekend and is a time when boating and sailing skills are challenged and reviewed by boating enthusiasts.

Fishing, scuba diving, and snorkeling are other popular sports. There is good game fishing for marlin, sailfish, and yellowfin tuna. Anglers from all over the world, but especially from the United States and other Caribbean islands, compete in the Spice Island Billfish Tournament that is held every January.

Grenada has some of the most beautiful beaches in the world. It is possible to wade into the sea and watch schools of fish in the clear blue waters. Even in the Carenage, an area where ships arrive every day to unload cargo, one can spot colorful reef fish. Coral reefs abound off the north, east, and south coasts of Grenada and the east coasts of Carriacou and Petit Martinique, and around the smaller islands of the Grenadines. It is no wonder that these islands attract many snorkelers and divers.

OTHER LEISURE ACTIVITIES

On weekends families often enjoy a picnic by the sea, or by a river or waterfall. Grenada has several lovely waterfalls: the Concord and Annadale falls in the parish of St. John, Tufton Hall waterfall in St. Mark, and St. Margaret falls in the heart of the Grand Etang National Park.

A Grenadian picnic is a simple affair. Almost everything that is required for a meal is available on the spot. Three stones form a triangle on which to put a pot, dry twigs and branches are placed underneath, and a fire is lit. Bowls, hollowed out of the calabash fruit, are the only containers needed, and a spoon is quickly fashioned out of a twig.

Hiking is another activity accessible to all. The central mountains, especially the Grand Etang National Park, has many well-developed nature trails. Mount Qua Qua provides the hiker with a wonderful view of the surrounding countryside.

Some people love to hunt. They shoot monkeys and armadillo. The meat of these animals is sometimes considered a delicacy.

Above: **Hiking through the Grand Etang National Park.**

Opposite: **Sailing in Grenada has a large following.**

A little boy happily playing with his toy yacht.

CHILDREN'S GAMES

Circle games were popular in the past. Two well-known examples of circle games that have come to us from the Caribbean are *Brown Girl in the Ring* and *Here We Go Loop-de-Lou*. These song games were played in school yards, at home with friends, or with parents and elders who taught the art of singing to the young.

On Carriacou similar songs called "pass plays" were sung by a circle of adults, most notably at wakes. Another is a *kalinda* or stick-fighting song. The stickman and his supporters sing a challenge to all to "meet me on the road."

Today children spend their time cycling with friends, playing soccer and basketball, or pitching marbles. Girls' enjoy jumping rope, jacks, playing baseball, and hopscotch. A popular game called *morual* ("MOR-u-al") involves drawing a rectangle in the dirt divided into eight or 10 sections. A ball is thrown, and the players move through the sections and try to gain control of as many of the sections as possible.

Some families gather in the living room to relax and watch television. If a home is without a television set, time is spent reading a book or talking and relaxing with friends under the shade of a large tree.

RELAXING WITH RUM

Men like to get together with their friends at the local rum shop for a "happy hour" of "eights" and a game of dominoes or cards. An "eight" is a measure of rum that is often drunk in one gulp or consumed a little more slowly and shared among friends. If one desires, the rum can be washed down with a glass of iced water. Dominoes is a game that is taken seriously in Grenada. The men form clubs that compete in a championship.

Grenadian men gathered for a game after lunch.

NIGHTLIFE

Nightlife in Grenada is picking up with the increasing emphasis on tourism. Two favorite nightspots around St. George's that are patronised by Grenadians are the Fantazia 2001 disco and the Sugar Mill in the Grand Anse area. This is where the music is "hot" and a steel band plays soca, reggae, and other Carribean music. Besides catering to the needs of the local population, these places also offer tourists a cultural cabaret, a chance to sample a little of the local culture and folklore.

The town of St. George's is rather quiet in the evenings. There is just one movie house, the Regal Cinema, which is open three times a week.

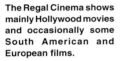

The Regal Cinema shows mainly Hollywood movies and occasionally some South American and European films.

FOLK TALES

Storytelling is a very important tradition in Grenada that springs from African roots. Folk tales are a means of teaching a people about their past, their culture, and the values of their society.

Story time often begins with someone calling out "Tim Tim" or "Crick Crack" to which the children would respond with "Papa Welcome" or whatever the local custom happens to be. Then everyone gathers around to listen to famous stories about the cunning of Anansi, the spider man. Anansi is half man, half spider, and is cunning, greedy, and shrewd.

In Anansi stories, small and seemingly weak animals are able to overcome strong and threatening ones like tigers and pythons by their wit and trickery. At the end of the tale it is customary for the storyteller to finish by announcing, "The story end and wire bend." The children are then treated to some food or drink. Anansi comes from the tradition of recounting folk tales, an art that developed during the days of slavery that brought great comfort to an oppressed people.

Besides Anansi stories, many other folk tales are about animals.

103

FESTIVALS

GRENADA HAS MANY FESTIVALS AND HOLIDAYS, but perhaps the most important and well-known occasion is Carnival. This is Grenada's annual national festival. Grenada shares this celebration with many other countries in the region, especially those with a Roman Catholic tradition, such as Brazil, Trinidad and Tobago, Jamaica, Barbados, and most of the other islands in the Caribbean.

As the majority of Grenadians are Roman Catholic, feast days in the Church calendar are also festival days. Many of these are movable feasts, that is, the calendar day on which it falls changes from year to year.

Grenadian festivities are marked by great feasting and drinking, laughter, music, and dancing that last throughout the day.

CARNIVAL

Historically, Carnival allowed people to have a big celebration before Lent, when they were required to fast. Carnival was their last chance to dance, sing, and make merry before the 40 days of the Lenten season.

When Grenada was a French colony, the planters celebrated this time with much socializing. They had dinners, concerts, and paraded in beautiful costumes. After emancipation in 1834, former slaves used Carnival as a vehicle to parody the planters. The masked players imitated estate owners and other important people, and this use of disguise enabled them to step over the boundaries of color and social class.

Above: **Flags in the national colors decorate the streets of St. George's during Independence Day.**

Opposite: **Participants in the costume parade of Carnival.**

Carnival is a time to dress up and join in costume parades. Grenadians look forward to its arrival every year.

Carnival has evolved over the years. The costumes and masquerades have been retained, but the mood is mainly celebratory. There are talent contests, steel band performances, and a search for the year's Calypso King and Carnival Queen. Grenada celebrates Carnival on the Monday and Tuesday of the second week of August, although the preparations begin long before then.

Carnival has retained a little more of its old flavor on Carriacou. Earlier this century Pierrots, or clowns with white faces, in each village would gather months before Carnival and challenge each other in wrestling and reciting Shakespeare. From these contests would come kings from each village who would all meet on Shrove Tuesday. Today this riotous celebration has been tamed into a contest among participants who dress as Pierrots, in long socks, lace skirts, and long sleeved shirts to recite perfectly from Shakespeare's *Julius Caesar*.

PLAYING MAS

A big part of Carnival is dressing up in costumes and masks or "playing mas," as Grenadians call it. Many of these costumes and characters have historic significance. The night before Carnival is traditionally devoted to mocking and driving out devils. Many of the masqueraders dress as *jab-jab* ("JAB-jab"), which is a Creole word for devil. They use body paint, grease, or molasses to color their bodies and dance in a pantomime that tells of their escape from hell to heaven. Sometimes the Carnival revelers dress to parody events of the past year.

Another traditional Carnival mas character is Pierrot, a clown-like entertainer with a white face, who usually wears a loose, fancy white dress. This dates back to

a time when itinerant minstrels would whiten their faces and wear long white dresses. Related to the Pierrot is the Short Knee. When former slaves were allowed to take part in the celebrations, they imitated the Pierrot character. They would travel from village to village challenging others in oratory. But beneath their long dresses, they hid weapons that they used when brawls broke out. When these long costumes were outlawed by the government, revelers took to wearing baggy pants that reached just below the knee, hence the name "Short Knee."

FEAST DAYS

Movable feasts are festival days that change from year to year depending on the liturgical calendar. Corpus Christi occurs eight weeks after Easter. It is celebrated with a special church service and street processions. Although it is a Roman Catholic festival, other churches join in the celebrations in a spirit of unity and ecumenism. This is reciprocated when the Anglican community celebrates the feast of St. George. Christians from the other churches join in the procession through the town of St. George's.

The Feast of St. Peter and St. Paul on June 29 is reason for another big celebration. It is called Fisherman's Birthday because St. Peter was a fisherman. Grenadians celebrate this festival because many of them come from fishing families.

Christmas was once celebrated with a traditional Maypole dance. Young girls, each holding one end of a ribbon that was attached to the pole, would dance around the pole, weaving in and out to create patterns with their ribbons. Dancing the Maypole is no longer performed, but Christmas is still a very special time of the year. Houses are thoroughly cleaned, new things replace the old, and everybody dresses in their best clothes to go visiting. Musicians go around caroling or serenading. Kitchens bustle with the enormous amount of cooking that needs to be done to ensure that anyone who passes by or steps in the door is feted to his heart's content.

PARANG

Parang, a festival that occurs the weekend before Christmas, is unique to Carriacou. Parang came to Grenada from South America via Trinidad. It grew out of the tradition of going from house to house caroling. Today it is less a celebration of Christmas, and has an identity of its own.

Parang songs in Carriacou are sung in English. Full of humor, the songs are often done impromptu and tell of someone's misdeeds. The festival was started more than 20 years ago, in 1977, by the Mount Royal Progressive Youth Movement, a nonprofit organization that wanted to celebrate this aspect of the island's culture.

The three-day festival begins with a Hosanna Bands contest—a carol singing contest among village groups. This is followed by a calypso and soca jam session. Performers from Carriacou and Grenada entertain a large crowd, and a foreign artist from Trinidad or Barbados is usually invited. Parang festivities reach a climax on the third night when bands playing only percussion instruments sing about *melee* ("ME-lee"), the political and other talked-about events of the year. If one does something scandalous, especially close to the month of December, one might be warned to "be careful, we go put you on the banjo!" Most songs are sung with a biting humor.

Names are sometimes linked with the rumors sung in the Parang songs. This has led to threats of legal suits against the singers.

Steel band members preparing for a performance.

BIG DRUM

Carriacou is particularly known for Big Drum. The festival is experiencing a revival, especially as young Carriacouans are renewing their interest in their heritage of African drumming and dances.

There are three drums: the center drum is called the cot drum; the two side drums are bula drums. Dancers and singers accompany the drums. The lead singer sings parables of troubles or repressions, warfare, and gossip. The songs tell of a longing for West Africa. Some lament the lives of the people or ridicule the oppressor.

Dancers are called forth by the beat of the drum and dance in a circle. The dances reflect the African heritage of the various peoples who came to the island—the Kromantin, Ibo, Mandingo, Chamba, Banda, Moko and others. The Kromantin Dance is the most significant because the Kromantins, originally from Ghana, were one of the first groups to come to Carriacou. Every ceremony opens and closes with the Kromantin Dance.

MAROONS

Associated with the Big Drum is Maroon, an especially big sacrificial feast. The Dumfries Maroon in Carriacou is a yearly affair. Several families, often related, will prepare food that is put on trays and then placed on both sides of the road leading to Dumfries. Some food is taken from each tray by specially appointed people and presented to the Big Drum people who perform in the evening. The rest of the food is offered to passers-by.

BOAT LAUNCHING FESTIVAL

Boat building has a long and important history on Carriacou, so there is a celebration when a new boat is to be launched. The ceremony begins with a Big Drum performance and a *saraca*, followed by a pouring of spirits and the sprinkling of rice around the boat. Animals are ritually slaughtered. Chickens are killed in the galley to symbolize an abundance of food, a ram goat is killed on the stern to bless the ship with fair winds, and a sheep is slaughtered over the bow to make steering easy. A second round of spirits is poured around the boat.

A priest is usually invited to bless the boat. He says his prayers and sprinkles holy water over the boat while accompanied by two people who represent the godparents of the boat. The culmination of the ceremony is the unfurling of a flag with the boat's name. Then, as the drums roll, the boat is released into the water for the first time. This is the important "cutting down" of the boat. Men all along the side of the boat use axes to cut the posts on which it rests. The boat is gradually lowered into the sea.

Boat launchings on Petit Martinique and Carriacou are day long affairs.

FOOD

THE CARIBBEAN IS A MEETING PLACE for many cuisines, such as African, Spanish, British, Dutch, French, Portuguese, Chinese, and East Indian. Grenadians have been able to match this rich heritage with a plentiful variety of fresh foods for the cooking pot. Add spices—for Grenada is famous for being the isle of spice—and the result is a cuisine that is varied, interesting, and unique to the island.

Slavery has left an important imprint on the country's cooking. The slaves, rooted in poverty, could not afford meat or fish. Instead they resorted to cooking with "ground provisions"—starchy root vegetables like yams, dasheen, and sweet potatoes. Beans, salt fish, and salt pork added some variety to their diet. Ground provisions remain an important part of the diet today, providing tasty substitutes for potatoes in the Grenadian diet.

Left: **Street vendors using traditional coal pots to roast corn. The coal pot used to be found in every Grenadian kitchen where it was used for daily cooking. Today its use seems to be limited to outdoor cooking, for example, during a fete when a little barbequing needs to be done.**

Opposite: **The Saturday Market in St. George's bustles with activity as shoppers bargain for their purchases.**

GROUND PROVISIONS

While the potato is a staple in Grenadian cooking, ground provisions are a popular substitute. Dasheen, tannia, eddoe, yams, cassava, and sweet potatoes may be steamed, boiled, or added to stews. There are also two members of the banana family that are equally versatile—the plantain, which looks like a large green banana, and the bluggoe, which is shorter and thicker in size. These rather starchy, solid, and bland fruits are often fried and eaten as a popular snack.

Another starchy item that often makes its appearance on the dinner table is breadfruit. This round, green fruit is cooked and eaten like a vegetable. Breadfruit is native to the Pacific Islands, and the story is that it was introduced in the late 18th century by Captain Bligh of *Mutiny on the Bounty* fame, to provide food for slaves. It is bland and chewy, but it absorbs the flavors of the spices with which it is cooked. Breadfruit balls are made by mashing the breadfruit, forming it into balls, and deep frying them. Breadfruit soup is made with salted meat and onions. Grenada's national dish, oildown, is made with breadfruit and meat, usually chicken or pork, cooked in coconut milk. A kind of heavy dumpling is added to the stew. Turmeric produces the characteristic yellow color of the dish.

ROTI AND RICE

After slavery was abolished, new groups of indentured laborers arrived in the region and brought with them new foods. The East Indians introduced curry powder and a thin pancake made of flour and water, called roti. The Chinese brought Asian spices and vegetables.

Grenadians have transformed the Indian roti and curry into something of their own. The pancake is made into a wrap and filled with a curry-flavored potato and meat mixture that is a meal in itself.

Rice, which was probably introduced by the East Indian and Chinese communities, is also popular. It is often cooked with pigeon peas and called "peas and rice." Alternatively, rice is cooked with spices and is then known as "seasoning rice." Pigeon peas, or yellow peas, may also be served on their own as a side dish, or cooked with salt beef and other meats and seasonings.

When the Europeans arrived, they introduced more new foods—wine, olive oil, cheese, salami, and European spices. They also brought bread. Slaves were taught by their planter families to make bread, but being used to ground provisions they made a heavier kind of bread. Today bread is found in many forms but most commonly as a kind of long roll or "French" bread, with a crusty surface. Bakeries make all sorts of bread—butter bread, French rolls made of a heavy, unleavened dough, as well as a lighter version leavened with yeast, and buns. People drop by the bakery during the day not only to buy bread but also for drinks and "pies," which are squares or triangles of pastry filled with meat, fish, salami, cheese, and jam.

A confectionery in the town of Tempe in Carriacou. Its cakes and pies are popular with workers looking for "lunch on the go."

ISLE OF SPICE

No discussion of Grenadian food can be complete without mentioning spices. The island is known as the "Isle of Spice," and for good reason. All kinds are grown here—cloves, cinnamon, ginger, vanilla, bay, turmeric (which Grenadians call saffron), pimento, pepper, nutmeg, and mace. These are used in many combinations to flavor all sorts of meat dishes, cakes, and sweets.

Chicken, pork, beef, and mutton are all part of the Grenadian diet. These are marinated with spices and cooked slowly. Marinating and seasoning are important elements in Grenadian cooking. Except for tender cuts of meat and quick-cooking foods like fish, hardly anything

A customer picking out scotch bonnets. A spice vendor's table at Market Square displays cinnamon bark in bundles, nutmeg, mace, cloves, and other spices.

is cooked without being properly seasoned and marinated for a few hours. The secret of spicing the food is to ensure that the taste of no one spice can be identified; rather the different spices should combine to produce a subtle blend of flavors.

THE PEPPER POT

Grenadians cook lots of soups and stews. The "one pot," a combination of vegetables, meat, and often seafood, makes a popular holiday lunch. A soup commonly found in restaurants is the thick, dark green callaloo soup. The callaloo is the tender leaf of the dasheen plant and looks and tastes like spinach. It is simmered in coconut milk and spices until soft.

Previously a plantation house, the Morne Fendue is a guesthouse located at Sauteurs, in northern Grenada. The guesthouse is famous for its pepper pot lunch.

The pepper pot is a special stew that can contain several kinds of meat. The most important ingredient is casareep, which acts as a preservative and is made from the cassava plant. It gives the stew a distinctive bittersweet taste. The pepper pot can last indefinitely, as the cook keeps adding more meat and vegetables to it even as it is consumed. Some pepper pots have been kept for more than 20 years.

Souse is a festive dish made with pig's feet. The feet are cleaned and boiled until tender. The meat is then sliced and combined with a sauce made from garlic, onions, lime juice, salt, and pepper. Seafood is often served for dinner. Conch, or *lambi*, is the most popular seafood delicacy.

Grenadian food, though well spiced and seasoned, is seldom chili-hot although the Caribbean is home to one of the world's hottest peppers, the Scotch bonnet. But there is usually a bottle of hot sauce on every restaurant table.

THE WORLD'S HOTTEST PEPPER

The West Indies produces the world's hottest pepper, the Scotch bonnet. The name comes from the crinkled crown of the pepper, which some believe looks like a Scottish bonnet. There are red, yellow, orange, or green ones. It is many times hotter than the jalapeño. The hottest part of the pepper is not the seeds, as some people believe, but the white veins that contain the capsaicin that is responsible for the fiery power of the vegetable.

It is difficult to understand what it is that makes the heat of the pepper such an attraction for people who live in hot countries. One theory is that it fosters perspiration, which is the body's natural cooling mechanism. Another is that there is a "high" that comes from eating hot peppers that makes those who love it want more. The body reacts to the pain caused by eating the peppers by producing endorphins, the same natural products that produces a "runner's high." Early European explorers found that if sailors ate peppers during the long sea voyages, they did not suffer from scurvy. Peppers are rich in vitamins A and C.

REFRESHING DRINKS

Fruit juices abound in Grenada—mango, papaya, golden apple (called June plum in other parts of the Caribbean), orange, avocado, guava, passion fruit, lime, banana, the five-finger fruit (also known as carambola or starfruit), soursop, and sweetsop (or custard apple).

Grenadians make juice with the most unlikely of ingredients. Even the sour tamarind is made into a deliciously tart drink. Ginger beer, which is nonalcoholic, is also extremely popular. Mawby is made by boiling pieces of a tree that is native to the Caribbean together with some orange peel and spices. This produces a dark bitter liquid that is diluted and sweetened and left to ferment for a few days. The resulting drink is reminiscent of licorice, leaving a lingering and slightly bitter, herbal aftertaste. Sea moss is a milky-sweet drink made from seaweed.

Sorrel is drunk during the Christmas season. It is made from the fleshy dark-red sepals of a small plant from the hibiscus family that is also native to the Caribbean. The sepals are picked and soaked in water with bay leaves, cloves, and cinnamon and then strained to make a dark-colored drink. The sorrel flowers only around December.

A common scene in the markets is that of vendors slashing off the top of coconuts. Coconut juice is popular with shoppers who, after some hours of shopping under the blazing sun, like to enjoy this cooling drink in the shade.

RUM

Rum is the alcoholic drink that is most associated with the Caribbean. Rum is produced from sugarcane, and there are as many kinds of rum as there are islands in the region. There are several rum distilleries on Grenada Island. The Dunfermline Rum Distillery in St. Andrew was built in 1797 and still operates with power from a watermill, while the River Antoine Rum Distillery still produces rum with methods that have changed little since the 1800s. The Grenada Sugar Factory and Westerhall Rum Distillery also produces its own rum.

Rum comes in many flavors and colors. The color of rum ranges from almost colorless to a dark brown. A light-colored rum is aged in ordinary oak casks, while a darker rum is aged in charred oak casks. Sugar caramel is sometimes added for color. Rum is also used in cooking and baking, and comes in many different cocktail concoctions. One concoction is rum punch, a drink that can be traced back to plantation days.

No mention of rum on Grenada is complete without mentioning Jack Iron, a rum so high in alcohol that if you put ice cubes in a glass of it they will sink to the bottom! This drink is most associated with Carriacou, where it is the island's special drink.

HOW TO MAKE GINGER BEER

Ginger beer used to be given to slaves on the estates so they could celebrate with a nonalcoholic drink. It is a popular drink in Grenada during Christmas and is served in most restaurants.

$^1/_4$ pound (550 g) ginger root
1 lime or lemon
3 cloves
5 cups water

Remove the brown outer skin of the ginger root and slice the root thinly. Add the juice of one lime or lemon, three cloves, and five cups of water. Bring it all to a boil for about five minutes so that the ginger flavor is extracted. Allow it to stand overnight, then strain the liquid and sweeten it to taste. Pour into a pop bottle and leave it for a few days until a little foam forms on the surface. When this happens, your ginger beer is ready to drink. Refrigerate it or serve it cold on ice for a wonderfully gingery, sweet, and refreshing summer drink.

Opposite: **A coconut vendor cuts a coconut with great skill.**

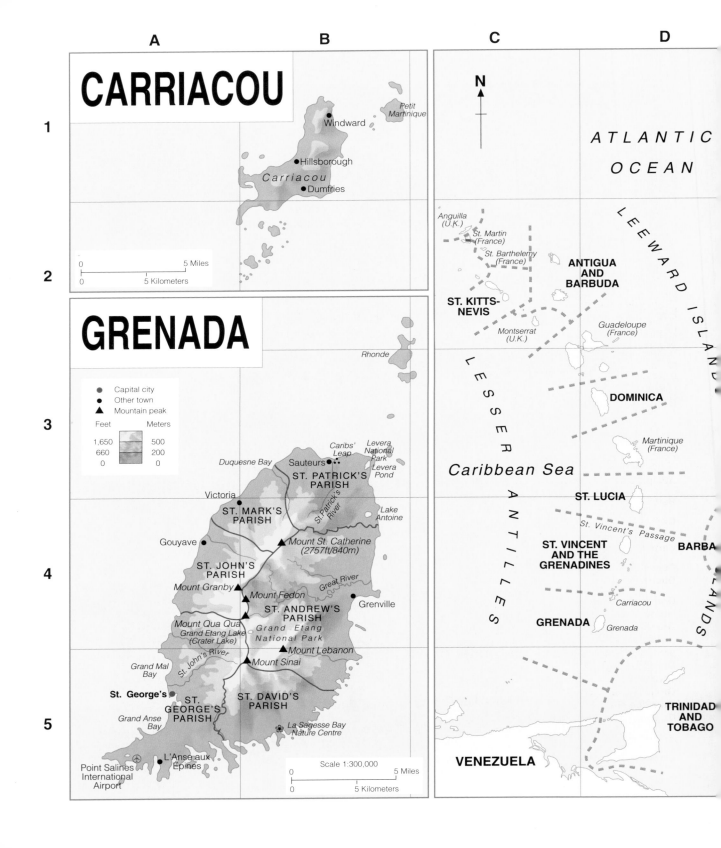

CARRIACOU

	A	B	C	D

1

Petit Martinique

Windward

Hillsborough

Carriacou

Dumfries

2

0 _____ 5 Miles

0 _____ 5 Kilometers

N

ATLANTIC

OCEAN

Anguilla
(U.K.)

St. Martin
(France)

St. Barthélemy
(France)

**ANTIGUA
AND
BARBUDA**

**ST. KITTS-
NEVIS**

Montserrat
(U.K.)

Guadeloupe
(France)

GRENADA

- ● Capital city
- ● Other town
- ▲ Mountain peak

Feet	Meters
1,650	500
660	200
0	0

Rhonde

3

Duquesne Bay

Caribs'
Leap

Levera
National
Park

Sauteurs

Levera
Pond

**ST. PATRICK'S
PARISH**

Victoria

St. Patrick's River

Lake
Antoine

**ST. MARK'S
PARISH**

Gouyave

▲ *Mount St. Catherine*
(2757ft/840m)

**ST. JOHN'S
PARISH**

Great River

Mount Granby ▲

▲ *Mount Fedon*

**ST. ANDREW'S
PARISH**

Grenville

Mount Qua Qua

*Grand Etang Lake
(Crater Lake)*

*Grand Etang
National Park*

4

St. John's River

▲ *Mount Lebanon*

*Grand Mal
Bay*

▲ *Mount Sinai*

St. George's ●

**ST.
GEORGE'S
PARISH**

**ST. DAVID'S
PARISH**

*Grand Anse
Bay*

*La Sagesse Bay
Nature Centre*

5

L'Anse aux
Épines

Point Salines
International
Airport

Scale 1:300,000

0 _____ 5 Miles

0 _____ 5 Kilometers

LESSER ANTILLES

Caribbean Sea

LEEWARD ISLANDS

DOMINICA

Martinique
(France)

ST. LUCIA

St. Vincent's Passage

**ST. VINCENT
AND THE
GRENADINES**

**BARBA
LANDS**

Carriacou

GRENADA

Grenada

**TRINIDAD
AND
TOBAGO**

VENEZUELA

Anguilla, C2
Antigua and Barbuda, C2–D2
Atlantic Ocean, D1

Barbados, D4

Caribbean Sea, C3
Caribs' Leap, B3
Carriacou, B1, D4

Dominica, D3
Duquesne Bay, B3

Gouyave, A4
Grand Anse Bay, A5
Grand Etang National Park, B4
Grand Etang Lake, A4–A5
Grand Mal Bay, A5
Great River, B4
Grenada Island, D4
Grenville, B4
Guadeloupe, D2

Hillsborough, B1

L'Anse Aux Épines, A5

La Sagesse Bay Nature Center, B5
Lake Antoine, B4
Leeward Islands, D2–D3
Lesser Antilles, C3–C4
Levera National Park, B3
Levera Pond, B3

Martinique, D3
Montserrat, C2
Mount Fedon, B4
Mount Granby, A4–B4
Mount Lebanon, B4–B5
Mount Qua Qua, B4
Mount Sinai, B5
Mount St. Catherine, B4

Petit Martinique, B1
Point Salines International Airport, A5

Rhonde, B2–C3

St. Lucia, D3–D4
Sauteurs, B3
St. Andrew's Parish, B4
St. Barthelemy, C3

St. David's Parish, A5–B5
St. George's, A5
St. George's Parish, A5
St. John's Parish, A4–B4
St. John's River, A5
St. Kitts-Nevis, C2
St. Lucia, D3–D4
St. Mark's Parish, A4–B4
St. Martin, C2
St. Patrick's River, B3–B4

St. Patrick's Parish, B3
St. Vincent and the Grenadines, D4
St. Vincent's Passage, D4

Trinidad and Tobago, D5

Venezuela, C5
Victoria, A4–B4

Windward, B1
Windward Islands, D3–D4

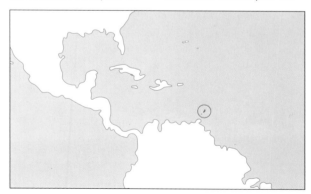

QUICK NOTES

OFFICIAL NAME
Grenada

LAND AREA
140 square miles (363 square km)

POPULATION
96,008 (July 1999 estimate)

CAPITAL
St. George's

ADMINISTRATIVE DIVISIONS
Six parishes, including St. Andrew, St. David, St. George, St. John, St. Mark and St. Patrick, and the dependencies of Carriacou and Petit Martinique

NATIONAL MOTTO
Ever conscious of God, we aspire, build, and advance as one people.

NATIONAL BIRD
The Grenada dove

NATIONAL FLOWER
Bougainvillea

MAJOR LAKES
Grand Etang Lake, Lake Antoine

CLIMATE
Tropical, with northeast trade winds

HIGHEST POINT
Mount St. Catherine (2,757 feet/840 m)

MAJOR RELIGIONS
Roman Catholic (53%), Anglican (13.8%), and other Protestant groups (33.2%)

CURRENCY
1 EC dollar (EC$)=100 cents.
Fixed exchange rate of US$1=2.7000 EC$

OFFICIAL LANGUAGE
English

INDEPENDENCE DAY
February 7, 1974

MAJOR INDUSTRIES
Food and beverages, textiles, light assembly operations, tourism, and construction

MAIN IMPORTS
Food, manufactured goods, machinery, fuel, and chemicals

MAIN EXPORTS
Bananas, cocoa, spices, nutmeg, fruit, fish, vegetables, clothing, mace, and flour

IMPORTANT GRENADIANS
Maurice Bishop (1944–1983), revolutionary
Junior Murray (1968–), cricket player
Slinger Francisco (1935–), Calypsonian

GLOSSARY

Amerindians
The original people who inhabited the Americas.

animism
The belief that spirits inhabit natural objects such as stones and trees.

colony
A territory that is distant from the country that governs it.

Creole
Also called patois, a language that is based on two or more languages.

emancipate
To set free from slavery.

emigrate
To leave one's country and settle in another.

federation
A union of several states.

gross domestic product
The total monetary value of goods and services produced in a country in one year.

indentured laborer
A person who is contracted to manual work.

jab-jab (“JAB-jab”)
A Creole word for “devil.”

jumby (“JUM-bi”)
Spirit of the dead.

Koran (“KOH-ran”)
The Muslim holy book.

lajabless (“LA-jab-las”)
Devil woman.

lambi (“LAM-bi”)
Grenadian word for conch.

obeah (“o-bia”)
Witchcraft.

playing mas
Dressing up in costumes and masks during Carnival.

petroglyphs
Prehistoric drawings or carvings on rock.

Rastafarianism
A religion that believes Haile Selassie, former emperor of Ethiopia, is God and that black people must return to their home, Africa, one day.

saraca (“SAH-ra-ca”)
Sacrificial feast.

Shango
An African religion with belief in many spirits.

BIBLIOGRAPHY

Bendure, Glenda and Friary, Ned. *Eastern Caribbean.* Victoria, Australia: Lonely Planet Publications, 1994.

Rogoziski, Jan. *A Brief History of the Caribbean: From the Arawaks and the Caribs to the Present.* USA: Facts on File, 1992.

Sinclair, Norma. Grenada, Isle of Spice. London:Macmillan Education, 1992.

Tramblay, Helene. *A House that Adna Built: A Family in Grenada.* Winnipeg: Peguis Pub. Ltd, 1997.

INDEX

administration, 17, 43
Africa, 18, 25, 26, 28, 29, 36, 53, 55, 57, 59, 76, 77, 79, 85, 88, 93, 110, 113
agriculture, 16, 43, 45, 62, 71
airport, 39, 51
Americans, 3, 39
Amerindians, 21, 22, 43, 54
Anglican, 74–76
Anguilla, 8
animists, 73
Antigua, 34, 50
Arawaks, 21, 23, 31, 53, 54, 73
architecture, 16, 75, 90
army, 39, 42
arts, 43, 85
Ashburton Treaty, 28
Asia, 36, 114
Atlantic Ocean, 8, 55

Bahamas, the, 8, 22, 50, 53
bananas, 43, 45, 46, 50, 56, 69, 114
band, 67, 85, 88, 102, 109
Barbados, 34, 42, 50, 70, 105, 109
beach, 3, 11, 12, 19, 45, 62, 64, 98
Big Drum, 59, 69, 110, 111

birds, 15, 54
birth, 61, 69
Bishop, Maurice, 33, 38, 41, 93
Blaize, Herbert, 33, 34, 36, 39
Boat Launching Festival, 59, 111
boats, 54, 62, 95, 111
Brazil, 105
British, 16, 18, 22, 23, 25, 26, 29, 30, 31, 33, 34, 35, 37, 55, 57, 59, 71, 74, 90, 95, 113
British Labour Party, 35

Calcutta, 57
Canada, 51
capital, 16, 74
Capuchins, 74, 75
Carenage, 8, 16, 85, 95, 98
Caribbean, 3, 7, 8, 10, 13, 14, 19, 21–23, 25, 26, 29, 34, 38, 49, 50, 51, 53, 55, 59, 61, 70, 71, 73, 77, 81, 85, 98, 102, 105, 113, 119, 120
Caribbean Community, 50
Caribs, 10, 18, 21, 23, 24, 31, 43, 53, 54, 73
Carnival, 59, 86, 105, 107
Carriacou, 7, 17, 18, 48, 51, 59, 70, 74, 98, 100, 109–111
cassava, 21, 54, 114, 118
Castro, Fidel, 38

children, 57, 59, 62, 66, 71, 76, 77, 91, 100, 103
China, 29, 113, 114
Christianity, 57, 68, 73, 75, 76
Christmas, 108, 109, 121
church, 18, 61, 74–76, 108
Church of England, 74
Church of Scotland, 75
Ciboneys, 21, 31, 53, 54
circle games, 95, 100
climate, 7, 9, 14, 18, 45
clothing, 49, 50, 54, 56, 58, 89, 107, 109
coast, 10, 12, 13, 18, 19, 28, 51, 54, 98
cocoa, 16, 18, 43, 45, 46, 50
colony, 16, 24, 28, 30, 35, 36, 73, 74, 75, 88, 93, 105
Columbus, Christopher, 21–23, 31, 54
Congress of Vienna, 28
constitution, 38, 39
Council of State, 34
crafts, 14, 43, 57, 85, 92
craters, 12, 16, 19
crater lake, 12
cricket, 59, 95–97
crime, 42
crops, 18, 43, 45, 46, 54, 56, 59

INDEX

Crown Colony, 29, 34, 36, 37
Cuba, 8, 13, 22, 23, 38, 39, 41, 53

dance, 59, 67, 85, 88, 95, 105, 110
death, 24, 28, 40, 61, 68
defense, 36
Denmark, 28
diseases, 28, 54
Dominica, 8, 25, 29, 34
drinks, 61, 105, 119, 121
drums, 85, 88, 89, 110, 111

earthquakes, 8, 75
East Indies, 22, 46
Eastern Caribbean Supreme Court, 42
economy, 24, 30, 34, 45, 58
education, 35, 58, 71, 95
elections, 39, 40
emancipation, 26, 29, 30, 31, 105
employment, 45, 65
England, 23, 28, 34, 36, 42, 51, 55, 89
English, 16, 58, 85, 89, 93
entertainment, 83, 93
Europe, 23, 51
Europeans, 15, 18, 21, 23, 26, 28, 46, 53–55, 73, 86, 115, 118
exports, 34, 43, 50

factory, 45, 46, 64, 65
family, 55, 61–63, 64–66, 68, 69, 99, 101, 108, 110
fauna, 13, 15
fish, 15, 21, 48, 50, 56, 63, 98, 113, 115, 116
Fisherman's Birthday, 108
fishing, 17, 18, 43, 48, 54, 59, 62, 98, 108
flora, 13, 14, 62
folk beliefs, 59, 68, 73, 76
food, 49, 50, 54, 56, 58, 69, 105, 110, 111, 113, 114, 118
foreign aid, 48
foreign exchange, 45

forts, 8, 26, 28, 31, 38, 74
France, 23, 28
French, 8, 16, 18, 22–24, 26, 31, 45, 55, 58, 59, 73, 74, 85, 89, 90, 105, 113
fruit, 14, 47, 50, 54, 56, 62, 99, 119

Gairy, Eric Matthew, 35, 38, 93
Gouyave, 17, 43, 82, 108
government, 18, 24, 29, 30, 33, 34, 37–39, 40, 42, 45, 57, 69, 70, 74, 75, 83, 95, 97, 107
governor-general, 34, 37, 39
Grand Etang National Park, 14, 19, 99
Greater Antilles, 8, 13, 53, 73
Grenada dove, 15, 43
Grenada Football Association, 97
Grenada National Party, 35
Grenada United Labor Party, 35, 40
Grenadines, the, 8, 17, 19, 24, 34
Grenville, 41, 63, 75
gross domestic product, 45, 50
ground provisions, 56, 69, 113, 114
Guyana, 50, 57

harbor, 11, 16, 26, 49, 51, 59
health, 40, 54, 70
hiking, 19, 43, 99
Hillsborough, 18, 74
Hinduism, 57, 76
Hispaniola, 8, 13, 22, 53
Holland, 23, 28, 55, 113
hospital, 69, 70
House of Representatives, 34, 37, 42
hunting, 15, 54, 59, 95
hurricane, 9, 10, 31, 46, 56

imports, 28, 50, 55
indentured labor, 29, 57, 114
independence, 30, 35, 36, 38
India, 29, 57, 113, 114
Indians, 53, 57, 93
industry, 24, 43, 48, 50
invasion, 31, 36, 39, 42
Islam, 57, 76
Jamaica, 8, 13, 23, 34, 50, 105

Japan, 48
judiciary, 30, 42

Kayaks, 59
kitchen, 62, 92, 109, 113

labor, 28, 33, 35, 54, 55, 57, 58
lakes, 11, 12
language, 58, 79–81
languages:
    African, 79
    Creole English, 79, 80, 82, 107
    Creole French, 79, 82
    English, 79, 86, 96, 109
    French, 79, 82
Latin America, 28
laws, 28, 29, 33
legislative council, 30, 33
Lesser Antilles, 8, 13, 53, 73
life expectancy, 70
literature, 82, 93, 106

mace, 47, 50, 116
Madras, 57
mangrove swamps, 13, 19, 43
manufacturing, 45, 50
marine life, 15, 54
market, 15, 18, 31, 45, 48, 61, 63, 64, 80, 91, 113, 114, 120
marriage, 61, 66, 77
meat, 54, 63, 69, 113, 114, 115, 116, 117, 118
media, 83
men, 19, 59, 63, 68, 69, 89
migration, 3, 13, 15, 29, 57, 59
military, 38, 41
missionaries, 74, 75
Mitchell, Keith, 39, 40
mosque, 76
Mount St. Catherine, 11, 19, 43
mountains, 8, 10, 11, 13, 18, 19, 23, 45, 95
music, 67, 83, 85, 88, 93, 102, 105

national bird, 15

INDEX

National Democratic Congress, 40
national flower, 14
New Democratic Congress, 40
New National Party, 36, 39, 40
newspapers, 83
nutmeg, 14, 16, 43, 45, 46, 47, 50, 116

Organization of Eastern Caribbean States, 38, 39, 41, 50

Parang, 59, 109
parishes:
St. Andrew, 11, 43, 70, 120
St. David, 43, 75
St. George, 43
St. John, 17, 43, 99
St. Mark, 43, 99
St. Patrick, 43
parliament, 36, 37, 40
People's Revolutionary Government, 31, 38
Petit Martinique, 7, 18, 48, 51, 59, 98, 111
petroglyphs, 21, 43
political parties, 33, 35, 39, 40
population, 18, 26, 28, 29, 34, 43, 53, 102
Portugal, 28, 29, 57, 113
prayers, 69, 111
president, 37, 38
prime minister, 33–35, 37–40, 93
Puerto Rico, 8, 13, 23

radio, 83, 85
rain, 10, 13, 17, 18, 46
rainforests, 11–13, 25
Rastafarianism, 76, 77
restaurants, 117, 121
rice, 58, 67, 115
River Antoine Rum Distillery, 25, 120
rivers, 10, 11, 17, 99
Roman Catholic, 74–76, 105, 108
Royal Grenada Police Force, 42
rum, 50, 101, 120, 121

schools, 57, 61, 70, 71, 75, 79, 100
self-government, 30, 33, 34, 36
settlers, 18, 22, 26, 45, 55, 74
slavery, 3, 21, 25, 26, 28–30, 55, 56, 58, 59, 74, 79, 86, 88, 113, 114, 115
soccer, 61, 95–97, 100
Spain, 3, 15, 22, 23, 28, 53, 113
spices, 43, 46, 47, 64, 113, 114, 116, 119
sports, 59, 83, 97, 100
St. George's, 16, 26, 31, 49, 51, 57, 63, 64, 70, 90, 102, 105, 108, 113
St. Lucia, 8, 24, 30, 34, 50
St. Vincent, 8, 17, 25, 29, 30, 34, 50
sugarcane, 15, 18, 21, 24, 25, 29, 46, 57, 59, 120

television, 59, 83, 95, 101
theater, 93
tourism, 45, 49, 65, 91, 95, 102
trade, 28, 45, 46, 50, 55
tradition, 18, 59, 61, 69, 109
transportation, 50, 51, 64
Trinidad and Tobago, 8, 13, 25, 29, 30, 34, 35, 50, 53, 57, 74, 75, 80 88, 105, 109

unions, 33, 35
United Kingdom, 50
United States, 3, 26, 31, 38, 39, 41, 42, 50, 58, 61, 70, 83, 98
university, 71

Venezuela, 8, 13, 23, 48
village, 11, 51, 57, 59, 61, 69, 91, 92, 107, 108
volcano, 3, 8, 12, 16, 19
vote, 30, 33, 36, 37

War of the Spanish Succession, 24
West Indies, 34, 96, 118
Windward Islands, 8, 11, 18, 26
women, 59, 62, 63, 65, 66, 68, 69, 89
World War I, 34

PICTURE CREDITS
Axiom Photographic Agency: 97
Bea Hunn: 65
Bes Stock: 42, 43
Camera Press: 30, 32, 38, 76, 83
Chris Huxley: 75
Dave G. Houser: 5, 11, 12, 16, 18, 19, 20, 37, 46, 49, 63, 77, 80, 110
David Simson: 10, 28, 119
Davon K. M. Baker: 4, 6, 7, 13, 14 (both), 17, 31, 54, 61, 67, 68, 82, 85, 89, 91, 98, 99, 103, 104, 106, 107, 111
DDB Stock Photo: 51, 88
Grenada Board of Tourism: 47, 92
Guek-Cheng Pang: 62, 73, 78, 79, 90, 93, 95, 101, 102, 113, 115, 116, 120
Hutchison Library: 3, 56, 64, 66, 70, 71, 100, 105
Jan Butchofsky/Dave G. Houser: 25, 53, 72. 74, 117
Lee Foster: 84
Neil Evans/GeoImagery: 8, 26, 108
North Wind Picture Archives: 21, 22, 23, 27, 55
Photobank: 60, 86, 112
Topham Picturepoint: 15, 24, 33, 35, 36, 39, 41, 44, 45, 52, 94, 96
Trip Photo Library: 1, 48, 50, 58, 123

ACKNOWLEDGMENTS
The author would like to thank Edwin Frank, Davon Baker, Patricia John, and all the many friendly and helpful Grenadians who spent time talking to her about themselves and their country.